RAISING WOMEN'S VOICES IN PREACHING THE GOSPEL

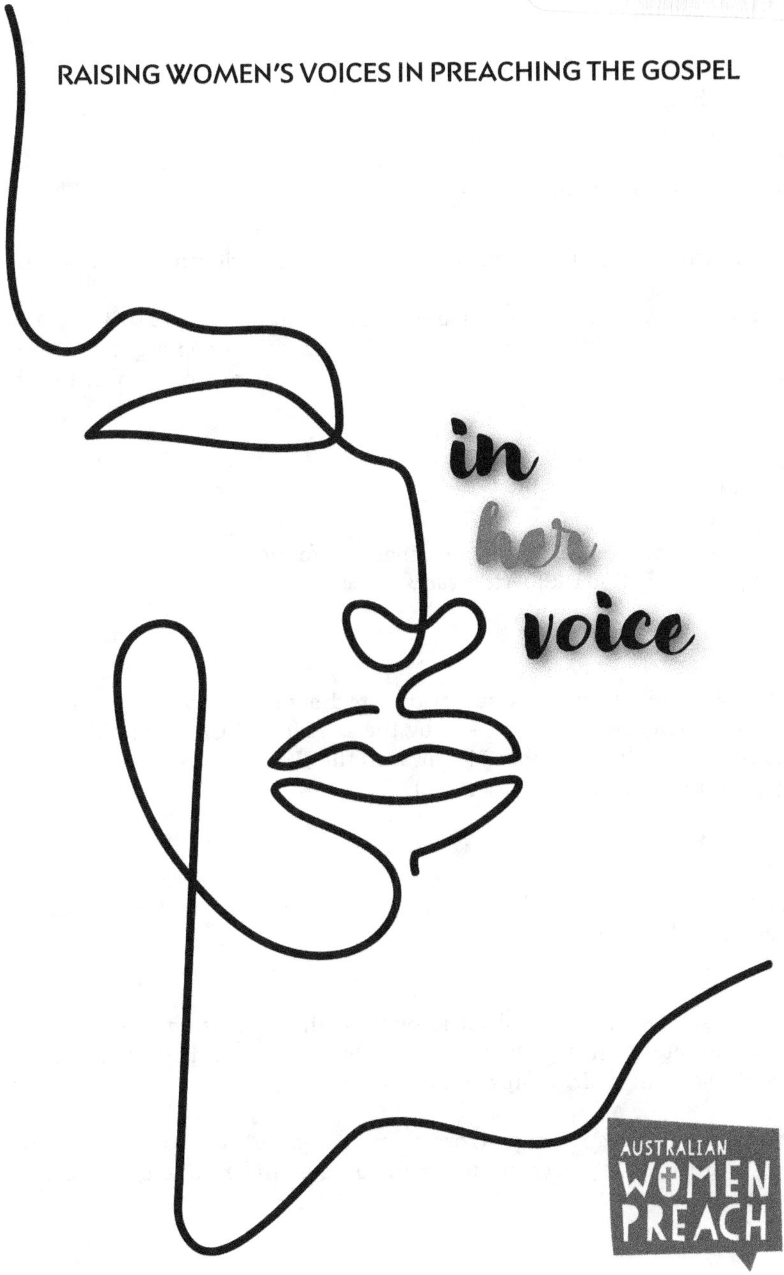

# in her voice

AUSTRALIAN WOMEN PREACH

garratt PUBLISHING

Published in Australia by
Garratt Publishing
32 Glenvale Crescent
Mulgrave, VIC 3170
www.garrattpublishing.com.au

Copyright in this work remains the property of the contributing authors.

Copyright © WATAC Inc. – Women and the Australian Church 2023
All rights reserved. Except as provided by the Australian copyright law, no part of this book may be reproduced in any way without permission in writing from the publisher.

Cover Design by Guy Holt
Text Design by Garratt Publishing
Edited by Juliette Hughes
Cover image © Sophie Cole, Lourde designer and founder
Artwork pp 1, 3 © Belinda Roberts, *Leaves on the Line*

Unless otherwise noted, scripture quotations are drawn from the New Revised Standard Version of the Bible, copyright © 1989 by the Division of Christian Education of the National Council of the Churches of Christ in the USA.
(Used by permission. All rights reserved.)

ISBN 9781922484581

Cataloguing in Publication information for this title is available from the National Library of Australia.
www.nla.gov.au

The authors and publisher gratefully acknowledge the permission granted to reproduce the copyright material in this book. Every effort has been made to trace copyright holders and to obtain their permission for the use of copyright material.

The publisher apologises for any errors or omissions in the above list and would be grateful if notified of any corrections that should be incorporated in future reprints or editions of this book.

# Contents

Welcome to Country ............................................................................ 1
DI LANGHAM & BELINDA ROBERTS

Preface .................................................................................................. 5
ANDREA DEAN

Australian Women Preach: an introduction ...................................... 7
TRACY MCEWAN

## The Journey: Advent to Resurrection

1. An Apocalyptic Invitation .............................................................. 11
Luke 21:25–36
KATECIA TAYLOR

2. Listening with the Ear of Our Hearts ........................................... 15
Luke 1:39–45
RACY SALVACION ESPINO

3. Lifted Up ......................................................................................... 19
John 3:14–21
JACQUI RÉMOND

4. Coming Home ................................................................................ 23
Luke 15:1–3, 11–32
MEL DWYER

5. Darkness and Light ....................................................................... 27
John 20:19–31
MELINDA JOLLY

6. Feed My Sheep .............................................................................. 31
John 21: 1–19
BETH DOHERTY

7. Love and Friendship ..................................................................... 35
John 15:9–17
DANIELLE ANNE LYNCH

## Tempus B

**8. Jesus Calms the Storm** .................................................................... 41
Mark 4:35–41
ELIZABETH LEE

**9. Jesus Invites a Woman to Preach** ..................................................... 45
Mark 5:21–43
PATRICIA GEMMELL

**10. Enough Bread Talk – I'm Outta Here!** ............................................. 49
John 6:60–69
CATHIE LAMBERT

**11. Be Opened** ....................................................................................... 53
Mark 7:31–37
FIONA DYBALL

**12. Original Love** .................................................................................. 57
Mark 10:2–16
MARY COLOE

**13. Through Jesus' Eyes** ....................................................................... 61
Mark 12:38–44
MICHELE CONNOLLY

**14. Staying the Course** .......................................................................... 65
Mark 13:24–32
RADHIKA SUKUMAR-WHITE

## Tempus C

**15. Part of Who We Are** ........................................................................ 71
Luke 3:15–16, 21–22
MONICA DUTTON

**16 Getting Real and Getting On With It** ............................................... 75
Luke 6:39–45
KATE ENGLEBRECHT

17. Jesus Visits Martha and Mary ................................................................. 79
Luke 10:38–42
GEMMA THOMSON WITH REFLECTIONS FROM
RILEY-JAYNE CARROLL & SAMARA SPADANUDA

18. What God Offers in Answer to Prayer ..................................................... 83
Luke 11:1–13
MOIRA BYRNE

19. Lighting Our Lamps and Standing With Those Who Have No Agency ... 87
Luke 12:32–48
CHRISTINE REDWOOD

20. 'I come to bring division' ........................................................................ 91
Luke 12:49–53
MICHELLE EASTWOOD

21. Gratitude ................................................................................................ 97
Luke 17:11–19
ANGELA MCCARTHY

## Celebration

22. Christmas .............................................................................................. 103
John 1:1–18
ALISON OVEREEM

23. Knowing, Being, Doing and Valuing ...................................................... 109
John 12:1, 12–13 • Luke 22:14
RACHEL MCLEAN, JENNIFER KING,
TAMILYN AH KEE & ASHLEIGH UNG

24. Celebration .......................................................................................... 115
Mark 16:15–20
ELIZABETH YOUNG

25. Empty Cross, Empty Tomb and Empty Space ...................................... 119
Luke 24:46–53
PATRICIA THERESE BENEDICT THOMAS

26. Trinity, Pentecost and Climate Change ..................................................123
John 15:26–27; 16:12–15
DI RAYSON

27. St Mary of the Cross MacKillop ..........................................................129
Matthew 6:25–34
ANGELA MARQUIS

28. On the Side of Truth ........................................................................133
John 18: 33–37
DI LANGHAM

MEET THE AUTHORS ..............................................................................137

ACKNOWLEDGEMENTS .........................................................................149

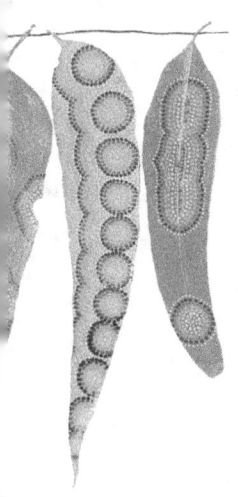

# Welcome to Country
## Revelation 22:2

DI LANGHAM & BELINDA ROBERTS

**... and the leaves of the tree
were for the healing of the nations**

I am a Boandik woman living in the lands of the Awabakal. My family history is that of dislocation, cultural annihilation, destruction of our lands, banning of our language and traumatic racism that included belittling our people as though we were worthless and useless. My history is not any different to that of many Aboriginal people in this land – it has left many scars.

In my community the women meet each week to paint gum leaves. They are dot-arted and placed in containers for families for Sorry Business and as gifts to family members. The leaves are collected, pressed and painted. They are then pressed again ready for distribution. We are an art therapy group, and the leaves not only look beautiful, but smell and feel beautiful as well.

*... and the leaves of the tree were for the healing of the nations...*

My daughter, Belinda, wrote the following words after dreaming she was at an art show with our leaves being pegged onto a clothesline.

'The tempest is an old-style clothesline with two long rows.
The ends are wood.
Pegged on the lines are my leaves.
I say we are here.
This is what's left.
We have been laundered, white-washed and hung out to dry.
Wood suspends us but they are not our trees.
Even the trees are off country.
We are not left out the front.
We are left out the back in the yard scattered,
needed but not considered.
We have our culture in small pieces,
fragments of an ancient rainforest
that is without canopy or roots.
Just left tormented by the sun and disconnected to the earth.
We are the leaves
We are the holes
We are the imperfections
We are the ochre and we are the artwork, untied, living,
holding the broken songlines.
We are different in size and shape and colour and form.
We are treated the same, we are tethered, hardened and left over time.
No smokings.
The cleanse came with the water,
polluted, white, soapy and unforgiving,
expected everything to make everything the same.
Us leaves left hanging out to dry.
Are we all supposed to be the same?
We are the women.
We are the grandmas.
We were taught to do the washing.
We are the ones hanging the leaves now.
When did we learn to do it ourselves?
When did we choose?
We need the washing now.
How else can we stay together?
We need those lines, that grid,

that way to live on a cycle that's foreign
in trees that aren't trees
on land we can only feel the stories of and listen to.

I am so sad that we are the caretakers now.
Why is our land so broken it needs us to separate
and hold ourselves in power and ownership
to decide its fate?
Why are we making choices for our land? We are not colonists.
We can't make that timber holding the lines grow roots.
Our ancestors are in that wood, in those trees,
in those buildings, in those churches.
We aren't and our leaves aren't.
People look at Jesus on the cross.
I see the nails driven into the trusses that hold up the roof.
I see all the nails in the roof in our ancestors
that protect us, shelter us.
We aren't so different and yet we are not the same.
What space is ours for our culture?
The backyard?
The church?
Is it in the language?
I don't speak it,
I feel it in me.
I am left out to dry.'

*... and the leaves of the trees were for the healing of the nations...*

Our leaves are for the healing of our nations. Our women paint them. We gift them. We use them for Sorry Business. Our smoking ceremonies use the leaves to heal and cleanse. The eucalyptus is a healing ingredient in all we do, and it comes from leaves.

In the beginning of the Bible, we have Genesis; we have the tree of life; and in the end of the Bible we have the tree of life in Revelation. Both have leaves. The leaves are the healing of nations. All nations.

# Preface

I'm proud to be president of WATAC Inc. (Women and the Australian Church) – one of the co-sponsors of the Australian Women Preach project. WATAC is an ecumenical organisation formed in 1983 by women and men of Catholic religious congregations to enable and advocate for a greater role for women in decision-making, ministry and leadership. Since that time, little significant progress has been made for women in the Catholic Church; although there have been occasional positives, such as the opening of the ministries of reader and acolyte to women.

Through initiatives such as Australian Women Preach, WATAC no longer waits for the Church to act, but seeks to model the Church we want to be: inclusive, diverse and welcoming. Our sisters from diverse Christian denominations have joined together, even when they can preach in their own churches. I am deeply grateful for their generous and inspiring homilies and for their solidarity.

On a personal level, the opportunity to contribute to Australian Women Preach was a challenge, but a delightful one. As I understand it, preparing a homily isn't meant to be easy. It is not a report. It is meant to involve a struggle with the text to break open the meaning. And not just any meaning – the meaning must be relevant to the experience of the community.

It costs me something to prepare a homily. I research, I harvest interpretations from scholars, I sit with the text, I wait for the gift or entry point in the text to emerge. As I invest myself in the task, the text begins to matter to me like never before.

Mary Oliver, a poet, uses the term 'to listen convivially' to describe this early stage of writing, where one is present and 'attending', warmly and openly, to the environment.

As the homily emerges, I try to balance genuine body or substance with a sincere, authentic voice with a spiritual purpose. The homily needs both continuity and uniqueness, grounded in the tradition of the Christian community and expressed with a fresh perspective.

Each time I write a homily it is like going on retreat. I review where I am in my spiritual life. I recentre myself on what is important. I grapple with the challenge of the text before I share it with you, my spiritual community. It matters to me that there is a community that invites me and permits me to witness to God's action in my life in this way.

Christian women are skilled at witnessing generously and faithfully to God in all kinds of contexts; they are missionaries, family members, professors, carers, authors, benefactors, contemplatives, mentors, advocates and so forth. But in some churches, including the Catholic Church, an insufficient range of voices is heard preaching at Eucharist. Women can preach but are not permitted to do so. Until that changes, I'm supporting Australian Women Preach, and I hope you will too.

*Andrea Dean,*
**President, WATAC Inc. – Women and the Australian Church**

# Australian Women Preach: an introduction

In late 2020 I received a phone call from Patricia Gemmell. Patricia explained that she had been awake well into the early hours of the morning pondering an idea: 'Could we create a podcast of Australian women preaching?'

The Holy Spirit moves in remarkable ways. As Patricia lay awake that morning, the Catholic Church in Australia was in the midst of a journey towards its fifth Plenary Council. The first phase of Listening and Dialogue was complete and the six Discernment Papers that were the fruit of the second phase of Listening and Discernment had been published. In the papers, written by small groups tasked with discerning the voice of the Spirit, all but one made strong statements about the importance of changing church culture to give women a much greater role in the Catholic Church. These papers identified the gifts that women could bring to governance, leadership, and decision-making, as well as pastoral and liturgical ministry within the Church.

At each step of the Plenary Council journey, Australian Catholics had been encouraged to continue discerning. It was in this spirit that Patricia and I spoke about the possibility of a podcast. We were inspired and emboldened by the recommendation made in one of the Discernment Papers, *Prayerful and Eucharistic*, to 'provide formal approval and encouragement for suitably qualified lay women and men to break open the Word'.

Initially, the task of creating a podcast seemed overwhelming. From our initial conversation we put the call out to the networks of WATAC (Women in the Australian Church) and The Grail in Australia. In response a small group of women gathered and the team behind Australian Women Preach was born: Patricia, Rebecca Beisler,

Elizabeth Lee, Angela Marquis, Colleen Rowe, Philippa Wicksey, Andrea Dean, and me, with Louise Maher as podcast producer.

Australian Women Preach was launched on International Women's Day, 8 March 2021, as a weekly podcast featuring Australian women preaching the Sunday Gospel. It was initially programmed to run for 30 weeks in the lead-up into the first assembly of the Plenary Council. However, two years later, the podcast continues to showcase the theological and preaching talent of Australian women.

It is with much excitement and anticipation that the Australian Women Preach podcast team brings you this book of reflections. First and foremost – through the podcast, and now this volume – we seek to raise women's voices and highlight the preaching talent of women. Inclusiveness and diversity are important, and the women who are featured in this volume come, so far as possible, from different Christian denominations, generations, backgrounds, cultures, and geographical locations. They all share a knowledge and love of the Gospel, and a Spirit-given desire to preach.

The Plenary Council presented the Catholic Church in Australia with an opportunity to listen and raise up the voices, wisdom, and insight of women. Unfortunately, during the final assembly the motion that would have instigated a process of change towards Catholic women preaching the homily during Sunday Mass was not passed. The Australian Women Preach podcast, and now this book, are providing platforms where women's voices can be heard outside rigid ecclesial structures.

Paul tells us in 1 Corinthians 12 that, in building up the Body of Christ, we are all called to discern our particular gifts and to use them for the good of all. Many Christian denominations embrace the gifts of women in ministry, and their faith communities are privileged to regularly hear these women preaching. We intentionally bring you their reflections alongside the words of women who are yet to be given permission to preach in their churches. We hope that you will be empowered by all these women as they give testament to the wonderful riches that can flow when women are allowed to preach.

*Dr Tracy McEwan,*
*On behalf of the Australian Women Preach team*

# The Journey: Advent to Resurrection

**THE JOURNEY: ADVENT TO RESURRECTION**
**1st Sunday Advent**

# An Apocalyptic Invitation
## Luke 21:25–36

### KATECIA TAYLOR

25 'There will be signs in the sun, the moon, and the stars, and on the earth distress among nations confused by the roaring of the sea and the waves. 26 People will faint from fear and foreboding of what is coming upon the world, for the powers of the heavens will be shaken. 27 Then they will see "the Son of Man coming in a cloud" with power and great glory. 28 Now when these things begin to take place, stand up and raise your heads, because your redemption is drawing near.'

29 Then he told them a parable: 'Look at the fig tree and all the trees; 30 as soon as they sprout leaves you can see for yourselves and know that summer is already near. 31 So also, when you see these things taking place, you know that the kingdom of God is near. 32 Truly I tell you, this generation will not pass away until all things have taken place. 33 Heaven and earth will pass away, but my words will not pass away.

34 'Be on guard so that your hearts are not weighed down with dissipation and drunkenness and the worries of this life, and that day does not catch you unexpectedly, 35 like a trap. For it will come upon all who live on the face of the whole earth. 36 Be alert at all times, praying that you may have the strength to escape all these things that will take place, and to stand before the Son of Man.'

I wonder what thoughts and feelings ran through your mind as you read this passage. It is a passage that can bring forth all kinds of emotions: from fear and confusion to comfort and hope.

I groaned when I read this passage, knowing I had to write a sermon on it, the one you are now reading. I wished for a simpler passage for the first week of Advent, some passage with some nice Wise Men, or angels singing to shepherds. Instead, this passage has wild imagery, violence and Jesus coming in on clouds.

However, as I sat with this text, read it repeatedly, looked to voices wiser than my own and wrestled and prayed with the text, I began to appreciate the opportunity to preach on it.

This passage of Luke falls into a genre we call 'apocalyptic.' What does that mean? Perhaps when we think of the apocalypse, we fear impending doom caused by climate change, or imagine big blockbuster movies. Perhaps the thing I am most certain of is that this genre of texts is a mystery.

Some folks say they have them all figured out. Many a cult has started around people who have cracked apocalyptic books, like supposed secret codes hidden in the Book of Revelation. Unfortunately, or fortunately, I have no secret code figured out. This short sermon cannot possibly provide you with all the answers to the questions this passage raises. Perhaps it may leave you with more questions than when you began.

I invite you to meet me in this mystery, because there I think God is. 'Apocalypse' in the Greek means, 'unveiling' or 'uncovering.' Let us see what we can uncover.

Nowadays, the apocalyptic genre, like this passage, is not super-popular, as are modern apocalyptic films, books and games. But this isn't that type of apocalyptic text. Apocalyptic texts talk about God coming down; they use imagery that is strange and needs interpreting or uncovering.

These writings were written in crisis situations – in exile or under oppressive foreign occupation. Whenever we look at apocalyptic texts, I think it is important for us to realise they are written by those without a lot of power in society, not the powerful. They acknowledge that sometimes it feels like the world is ending. Terrible things are happening; we are filled with anxiety and fear and we feel powerless.

But this passage says 'have hope', because redemption and deliverance are on the way and God is near amid the big things happening in the world.

Apocalyptic texts point us to God, amid life's biggest and scariest moments. Look up for a moment to see the 'Son of Man coming in a cloud with power and great glory.' Luke echoes words from the Book of Daniel 7:13:

> As I watched in the night visions, I saw one like a human being coming with the clouds of heaven. And he came to the Ancient One and was presented before him.

In Daniel's image, the one 'like a son of man' can be seen as representing the people of God. The coming in a cloud is not God coming down to earth on a cloud in Luke's version, but the opposite. Humans are coming before the Ancient One, God. But God in Luke's version comes to us. God's presence comes amid all that is happening. Yes, big scary things are happening but the text cries 'Look, God is here!' Jesus is present and all hope is not lost, the kin(g)dom of God is nearer than you think.

I think this text invites us to look up and lift our heads, for our hope is drawing near. If we look at Jesus in the gospels, we learn that our deliverance comes powerfully and in the unlikeliest of ways. Some folks interpret this passage to mean that Jesus will return to earth literally sitting on a cloud and judge who is a good Christian to be taken up to heaven and everyone else will be left out. But the apocalyptic genre was never written to be interpreted so literally or individualistically. New Testament scholar Bill Loader puts it this way: 'In the same way the liberation may be less the appearance of the Christ on the clouds and more the rising of the Spirit of Christ in renewal and global transformation.'[1]

What if this passage is an invitation to look up and around for the ways in which Christ's Spirit might be at work and also to do the Spirit's work? What if the Apocalypse is now? Look around – there are more famines, wars, people displaced, than ever. For many people today is the Apocalypse. Every day is the Apocalypse.

We all experience apocalyptic events. For many of us, with the pandemic, natural disasters, refugee crisis or personal loss, the

Apocalypse feels less mythical and more like our present reality. We have prophets crying out that the world as we know it will pass away if we don't respond to the climate crisis.

If the Apocalypse is now, what do we do? How do we respond in an apocalypse? How do we bring and be the Good News to people who cry out as their world is ending? Luke says we need to be on guard and alert. We should try to look up and find God. And where is God? God is in the unlikeliest of places. God is giving hope to those who feel totally powerless, God is with those whose worlds have just ended and there we are called to be also. God, peace, hope, love and joy are always seeking a home. So let us watch for the ways we might be Christ's loving presence. Let us prepare our hearts and minds to accept the many ways in which Jesus might be made present among us.

Apocalypse is a wild invitation. It is an invitation to not wait for some dramatic coming of Jesus but to join in Jesus' work now. Feed people, protest injustice, love with abandon, comfort people, be radically generous, side with those who are marginalised by society and take care of the world that God has given us. Look up, God has come and is coming in big and small ways – in neighbours, friends, people you don't expect – and in you.

## NOTES

1. Loader, W, sourced at https://billloader.com/LkAdvent1.htm on 8 December 2022

*THE JOURNEY: ADVENT TO RESURRECTION*
*4th SUNDAY ADVENT*

# Listening with the Ears of Our Hearts
### Luke 1:39–45

RACY SALVACION ESPINO

I remember my first trimester while expecting both my children. I was feeling so sick, hating the smell of certain foods – morning sickness was an everyday thing. I was concentrating on my needs and not paying attention to others.

But not Mary. According to Luke 1:39, '...(She) set out and went with haste to a Judean town in the hill country.' 'Set out' means to rise up and begin a journey, while 'haste' means 'in a hurry'.

Why is Mary in a hurry?

When the angel informed Mary that her child would be the Son of God, she said Yes – be it done according to thy will. Accordingly, Mary became the first follower of Christ and the Holy Spirit came upon her, filling her with overflowing wonder. Her first reaction was to jump up, dazed but reaching out to another person.

How often do we jump up and reach out to others, like Mary?

Let's look at Elizabeth before Mary's arrival. Remember, back then, there's no Messenger, no emails, no instant communication at all.

Elizabeth, an old lady, was six months pregnant. She lived in a silent house and had many questions for her husband, but he suddenly couldn't speak. Elizabeth doesn't know what the angel told her husband in the temple. How did her pregnancy come about? So many unanswered questions. Imagine Elizabeth's mental torture – bursting with curiosity, no Google to ask, hoping and praying for some sign from God.

(I can relate to Elizabeth at this point. Earlier this year, I nearly had a nervous breakdown. After several sessions with my spiritual director and counsellors, praying and discerning, I resigned from my previous role. I was blessed that I had good support.)

Then, one day, Elizabeth hears a new and unexpected voice. Imagine the scene. Mary was exhausted from her travels, worried about her cousin's health but super-excited to see the baby bump and witness this marvel the angel had described. Finally, sounds of joy filled the house.

Luke 1:41 states that when Elizabeth heard Mary's greeting, the child leaped in her womb. And Elizabeth was filled with the Holy Spirit.

No words were needed. The leap in Elizabeth's womb made her realise that Mary is also expecting – another impossible pregnancy. Mary's pregnancy is also an impossible one. Through the Holy Spirit, the baby's movement felt like pure joy!

The Holy Spirit is the binding power that attaches us in love and compassion to one another. The Holy Spirit reveals the invisible and seemingly unrelated connections to demonstrate the ties that bind us together with Christ.

And then the two women embrace.

In our COVID world, we have been longing for this physical contact but I can't return to Manila due to border closure: to the tight embrace from my mum who is unwell or to physically attend my nephew's baptism to act as his godparent.

Elizabeth's skin is still warm from the loving embrace of her young cousin. Overflowing with delight, she stands and looks at Mary. What words could possibly describe this moment? Without hesitation, she exclaimed loudly, 'Blessed are you among women, and blessed is the fruit of your womb.' (Luke 1:42)

I recently shared a Facebook post with my girlfriends that said, 'Shout out to women who smile at and compliment other women.' Wow, Elizabeth didn't just compliment Mary – she praised her, and praise is the soul of our faith.

To this day, we are one with Elizabeth in proclaiming Mary as 'Blessed'. We praise her every time we pray the rosary. How powerful is that?

And, finally, Elizabeth asked a question – why has this happened to me, that the mother of my Lord comes to me? (Luke 1:43) Just like my son when he was two years old, questioning, 'Why? Why? Why?'

When something bad happens to us, we also ask God why. Why not?

Elizabeth asked this question when she experienced something amazing and incomparable. These questions remind us we are alive, that we depend on God. The life of God's faithful follower is not a straight path – the journey not guided by human terms but by questions. Our sole purpose is to listen to the One whose intention is a mysterious plan for heavenly unity fulfilled in Jesus Christ.

In the silence of our hearts, God speaks. How often do we sit still and spend time with Him? Elizabeth continued: 'For as soon as I heard the sound of your greeting, the child in my womb leaped for you.'

Inside the womb, John already recognised Jesus' presence. He knew his destiny was intimately connected to the Lord's. John did not swerve from his mission to 'go before the Lord to prepare his ways'. That first leap was John's yes to the role God offered him – to be the 'prophet of the Most High'.

Are we true to our mission, like John, or are we getting sidetracked?

And blessed is she who believed that there would be a fulfilment of what the Lord promised.

Why was Jesus born? Because Mary believed. Mary's whole story resides in the expression that she is 'blessed' because she has 'believed.' Mary gives birth to Jesus. It is through a physiological process, but essentially the Son is a child of Mary's faith.

Abraham's story may assist us to grasp this better. How did Isaac come to birth? Genesis 18:9–15 states the promise of his birth is offered to Abraham. Same with us. God offers an invitation and never an imposition. We can choose to accept or decline. Abraham could have said, 'No, this is not possible', shutting the door to God's power to give life to Isaac. But Abraham said, 'Yes', accepting the promise of faith and opening the door for God. He became an improved version of himself, worthy of procreation. Truly, Isaac is the son of Abraham's faith in God.

I vividly remember the first time I held my daughter after hours of labour. This is comparable to when Abraham held his son and realised that he was the fruit of his faith — fruit he could see and touch in the person of Isaac.

This same thing happened to Mary. She received the invitation, questioned it but said 'yes'. The child she gave birth to was, above all, the fruit of her faith that the Lord would fulfil his promise.

Bottom line, what are the takeaways from this reflection?

I found three — Question, Listen and Respond.

## TAKEAWAYS

### QUESTION

It is alright to ask questions. Through inquiring, we open up what is bothering us, exposing our vulnerabilities and acknowledging that we don't know the answer and we are ready to hear another side.

### LISTEN

Listening with the ears of our hearts. We have to be on the look-out for the Lord's invitation and what He is telling us. Listening can be nourished by constant communication with Him through prayer. Spending daily quiet time listening to Him can sometimes be very challenging especially with the busyness of life — but we must persist.

### RESPOND

Like Abraham and Mary — God offers us an invitation. It is up to us to say YES and accept the promise of faith.

Are you ready to set out and go with haste?

*THE JOURNEY: ADVENT TO RESURRECTION*
*4th SUNDAY LENT*

# Lifted Up
## John 3:14–21

### JACQUI RÉMOND

In the third chapter of John's Gospel, we learn that Nicodemus, a leader of the Jews, goes to Jesus at night-time because he recognises that 'no-one can do these signs that you do apart from the presence of God' (v.2). Nicodemus expresses a sense of awe at Jesus, but he does not approach him in daylight where they might be seen. Potentially there may have been some jealousy or suspicion and a challenge to Jesus who senses a testing of his power and knowledge. Jesus responds by saying, 'Very truly, I tell you, no one can see the kingdom of God without being born from above' (v.3). Nicodemus inquires in a very literal way, asking 'How can anyone be born after having grown old? Can one enter a second time into the mother's womb and be born?' (v.4). How often do we fail to grasp what the story is about?

God is ever present in, with and through all creation – energetically holding and transforming creation. Jesus names physical and spiritual elements of birth: flesh, water, spirit and wind (vv.6&8). Jesus says, 'If I have told you about earthly things and you do not believe, how can you believe if I tell you about heavenly things?' (v.12). Jesus shares with Nicodemus that the material presence of God's creation is a real way for coming to understand God through our senses, which stimulates our faith. Jesus makes clear that believing in the Divine Presence of God in all creation creates real pathways for coming to know our loving Creator and ourselves in new ways. Jesus is inviting us to see that by being in close relationship with creation our understanding of God becomes transformed, and so does our own life.

In John 3:14–15 we hear, 'And just as Moses lifted up the serpent in the wilderness, so must the Son of Man be lifted up, that whoever believes in Him may have eternal life'. This story is about being given new life or a new way of being. Being born anew is another way of seeing that our faith journey of life on Earth is an ongoing invitation to conversion in Christ, which is always in dynamic relationship with Creation. When we open ourselves up to see the whole context of creation in Christ, we can see that we are called together, with God's Creation, to share eternal life. Perhaps we can also see that our whole human life, from conception to death, is a journey of ongoing turning towards God with all creation, also known as ecological conversion.[1] Our salvation through eternal life is physically and spiritually interconnected to our relationships with God and God's creation. Creation itself is an active agent of God's love. Millions or billions of agents all in one symphony or song of life, through which we are constantly relating to our Creator and Creation, but sadly, not always in life-giving ways.

There are parallels between the Moses story and the Jesus story that might help us see the eternal journey and how our choices can become more life-giving. We are living in a time of the COVID pandemic. This health crisis is nested within the broader ecological crises of climate disruption and the interrelated crisis of biodiversity loss, increasing pollution and poverty. For example, our human family is encroaching on wildlife habitats where zoonotic diseases from creatures, such as bats, are crossing into human bodies. In both Moses and Jesus stories, the people were in danger of death because of their sin. In both Sacred Scripture stories, God provided an agent of salvation: the bronze serpent in the first story and the Son of God in the second. The agent of salvation is 'lifted up' in both stories. People are saved by looking at or believing in God's agent of salvation. However, there are also a couple of significant differences between the Moses story of the bronze snake and the Jesus story.

The bronze snake is literally a piece of bronze, having no saving power in and of itself. When the Israelites began to make offerings to the bronze serpent, treating it as an idol, it was destroyed. Jesus, however, is invested with saving power. Looking at the 'lifted up' bronze snake gave the Israelites new life on Earth. Looking upon the 'lifted up' Jesus gives eternal life. Reflecting on these two agents of salvation, and noting that both are material, tangible realities within creation, some questions emerge. What is God providing for us as the material agent of salvation today? What is it that we are being called to 'lift up'?

Before answering these questions, it is important to notice that Jesus' message is inclusive – that 'whoever believes in Him may have eternal life' (v.15). This invitation is for everyone, not just the Israelites, but for every person and for all creation, which Jesus makes abundantly clear in the following verse. 'For God so loved the world that he gave his only Son, so that everyone who believes in him may not perish but may have eternal life' (v.16). What does this mean to you? Is it about having eternal life, a life everlasting personally? That would certainly be a gift, to live life that is everlasting! We tend to think of 'eternal life' as life without an end. However, this message also refers to a quality of life lived in the presence of God. And where is God present? God is present in the whole of the cosmos, including ourselves as creatures of Creation. What kind of relationships are we being called into with this presence of God in creation, as Cosmic Christ, resurrected in and with all creation? How do we share our life with Christ who is present in all creation? Are we being called, in this time of ecological crisis, to 'lift up' life itself? Life, which is always in communion with Christ, with our Creator and with the Holy Spirit?

The final verse brings some clarity to the story of salvation, and it wakes us up to the potentiality that we might be lifting up things that are not supporting life, for ourselves, for future generations of people, and for God's future creation. God sends Jesus not to condemn the world, but to save it. We ought not to take the gift of God's Son lightly. It was an enormous, costly gift for God to give, with plenty of divine sacrifice along the way considering the 13.7-billion-year journey of the universe so far, including the four billion years of Earth's evolution, and two hundred thousand years of human evolution that preceded Jesus' birth. We ignore the gift of Jesus and the gift of creation at our own peril. Jesus is with us, holding open the door to the Kingdom of God, so that we can join in the salvific dialogue with Christ.

Again, it prompts questions, such as: What are we 'lifting up' to the children of today? What are we 'lifting up' before creation around us? And ultimately, what are we offering up in who we are, and how we live with God? Each day when we wake up, we are presented with God's love in creation all around us. The daily choices we make are essentially what we're holding up to God – from the food we eat, our choice of transport, our way of relating and what we attend to each day. Is it our faith, our intentions and actions, or God's grace that determines our salvation?

It is all of these things. In Pope Francis' encyclical *Laudato Si*[2], we are being called to actively care for creation for our own sakes, for the future generations of creation and according to the Spirit. Paul says that the fruits of the spirit are love, joy, peace, patience, kindness, goodness, faithfulness, gentleness and self-control. Living in the spirit and the light of Christ, we are called to see and 'lift up' the diverse gifts of creation within the Cosmic Christ. We are called to be faith communities who actively lift up creation so that God's transformative action continues to re-birth new life through us and on Earth.

## NOTES

1. Pope John Paul II, Vatican General Audience, Wednesday 17th January, 2001.
2. Pope Francis, *Laudato Si' On Care for our Common Home*, 2015.

*THE JOURNEY: ADVENT TO RESURRECTION*
*4th SUNDAY LENT*

# Coming Home
## Luke 15:1–3, 11–32[1]

### MEL DWYER

The Parable of the Prodigal Son, Luke Chapter 15:1–3, 11–32, is one of my favourite stories in scripture. I love how Jesus provides the example of the father's immense generosity, compassion and mercy to teach us about who God really is.

The parable begins with the request of the son in Chapter 15:12 – 'Let me have the share of the estate that will come to me'. Through this request, the youngest son is in effect saying to the father, 'You are dead to me'. He is breaking relationship in the most significant way possible. Having cut himself off, the son takes his life in his hands and leaves for a distant country.

What remains significant in this journey of the young son is not so much the wild life that the son engages in, but rather the point where he realises that all the parties and money and drinking don't fill him, but instead leave him feeling emptier than ever. Reflecting on his actions, the younger son regrets his choice and instead of becoming burdened by this guilt, uses his regret to learn from his mistakes.

And so he comes home ...

Whatever our journey of faith looks like, self-awareness, striving to understand why I do what I do, is so important.

As I reflect on the character of the young son, it's tempting to compare ourselves and for me to say that this individual was a huge sinner; I've never left home nor asked my parents for my inheritance... And yet each of us is left to consider how many times we distance ourselves from God, even with being overly busy doing 'good things'.

How many times do we take our life in our own hands, trying to control things and forgetting that God is in charge? How many times do we try and fill the emptiness we experience with things that leave us unsatisfied?

As I reflect on my own life, there are some significant moments when I have been the prodigal daughter. I remember when I was a child, my grandmother would always call early on a Sunday morning. Every week she would ask me two questions: 'Have you been to Church?' and 'Have you been good to your mother?' Most of the time, the answer to both of these was no. I remember Mum trying many times in vain to drag me to Church as a teenager, and yet despite my grandmother's constant pleas, I found Mass boring and didn't know who I was or – whose I was – at that point in my life.

Then one day I returned from a sporting competition to the news that my faith-filled grandmother had lost her battle with depression and taken her own life. I realised then that something within me was missing. In reflecting on the inspiration of my grandmother's life of simple faith, I realised that filling my life with relationships and the competitiveness of elite sport were not filling the void in my heart, and that only God could do that. And so, like the prodigal son, I came home. I came home to discover a personal relationship with God who loves me as I am, not as I want to be. I came home to realise that my heart was made for love without limits and that I wanted to make a difference with my life by serving God as a consecrated woman.

And God ran to meet me, and continues to run to meet me every day, in the highs and the lows, promising me that He is with me, and that from death and darkness there can be life and light – if only I focus on God.

We see the image of a merciful father at the moment when the father sees the younger son returning in the distance. Hiking up his robes, the father runs to his son. Again, putting this gesture into the historical context, no respectable Jewish man would bare his legs and run...the father disregards all that is 'expected': he doesn't care what people think of him. He hitches up his robe and bolts to greet his son. Not with demands of explanation, not with words of 'I told you so': just with welcome ... just with love.

Here stands a powerful reminder for each of us. Despite making unwise choices in life and at times turning our backs on God, God continues to remain faithful, patiently waiting for our return.

It would be remiss to reflect on this parable without considering the third character in the story – that of the older son. As the younger son returns and is embraced by the father, we are confronted with the resistance and jealousy of the older son. In verse 29 he accuses his father: ' ... all these years I have slaved for you and never once did you give me anything ... '. There are powerful challenges for us in the life of the older son. We are invited to consider: how often do we compare ourselves with others? How often when we see things happen do we stand back and observe, not wanting to engage, or to forgive, but being so quick to judge?

The parable ends leaving us in suspense: we do not know what the elder son decided to do. Did he come in and join the celebrations, or did he stay distant and jealous? Therein lies an entry point for us. It's an opportunity for us to consider, at this point of our lives, what character are we in the Gospel? I've had moments when I've been all three of these characters – getting stuck in negative behaviours, hungering for mercy and forgiveness and believing I don't merit it. At the same time, sometimes I find myself standing on the outside of situations and being quick to criticise others. Yet, each one of us is called daily to be people of forgiveness. We are called to step out of our comfort zone, reveal our vulnerability, even at the risk of shaming ourselves – and run to those who need us most.

Undeniably Jesus told the story of the prodigal son for a reason. It says to us all: never mind what you've done. Just come home.

Just like the older son, as individuals and as a Church we need to get in touch with ourselves and with a God who is more merciful, more healing and more loving than we can understand. Our human frailty and vulnerability give us an opportunity to move beyond self-righteous rigidity. We need to go to God, seeking His mercy and knowing our deep need for God alone, conscious that relying on our own capacity we have failed and will continue to fail. God does not need our capacity: God needs our availability and our willingness to get up again and again every time we make a mess. And when we realise that we are not who we are because we are any better than anyone else, but because of God's mercy and God's grace, then perhaps we can become a little more accepting of the differences of others, and a little more ready to not just welcome but accept all people at the table with our actions, not just with our words.

It is not enough to do good. We have to do the Gospel. And just as Jesus sat with prostitutes and tax collectors, we need to ask 'Who are the prostitutes and tax collectors of 21st century Australia?' How do we make sure that in a meaningful way they feel valued, welcomed and affirmed for who they are, as they are, not as we want them to be?

Let us pray for the grace to be self-aware enough to learn from our mistakes. And let us pray for the capacity to choose courage over comfort on our journey to being at home with ourselves: at home with our vulnerabilities, and with our desperate need for the mercy of God who beckons us on in hope of who we are, and hope of who we are called to become, with God's unmerited grace.

NOTE

1. All biblical references from the *New Jerusalem Bible*.

*THE JOURNEY: ADVENT TO RESURRECTION*
*2nd SUNDAY EASTER*

# Darkness and Light
## John 20:19–31

### MELINDA JOLLY

This reflection is on John 20:19–31[1]. This piece of scripture is about the experiences of the disciples of the risen Lord according to John. The Gospel of John is one that people either love or hate; there do not seem to be many who fall in a middle ground. I happen to be in the category of loving it. I certainly have not always loved it, until I studied the gospel many years back and had an amazing teacher who opened the wonders of this piece of theological writing for me. I was fascinated by my lecturer highlighting the elevation of women in the gospel. To read the gospel in this way surprised me.

John's Gospel is a truly extraordinary work. He weaves themes and ideas throughout the book and some of them are present in this pericope. One of John's themes here is about darkness and light. The more I read the gospel of John, the more I realise there is nothing in this gospel that is a simple statement – there is meaning and depth behind everything.

This reading begins by stating it is the evening of the same day. The 'same day' the evangelist is referring to is the day Mary Magdalene becomes the first witness to the resurrection (Jn 20:16). Both Mary's encounter with the risen Lord and the disciples' encounter happens during the evening – it is dark. It is hard to imagine today how dark it would have been then; our nights are filled with artificial light that was not available to the disciples of the first century. Being fortunate enough to go out into the bush in Australia, I know that it really gives a glimpse of true darkness – darkness in which it is extremely difficult to see anything.

This is the kind of darkness John is referring to, but in a spiritual sense. It indicates that although the disciples had long been followers of Jesus, they still did not get what he was teaching. By having an idea of how dark it is, it shows even more just how much the disciples did not understand it. The disciples were best placed to fully grasp the mission Jesus had from the Father, but they were still in the dark. To grasp the mission, to come to the light, they had to experience the Risen Christ. They each had to come to a realisation, a transformation, to be able to understand. In this sense it represents everyone's own journey of faith. Faith in the Father, Son and Spirit – or Creator, Word and Spirit – deepens over time, often during particular transformative life experiences when we each have our moment of coming from spiritual darkness into the light.

This text highlights how important it is that each of us comes to the light in our own way and time. Mary Magdalene went to the disciples to tell them of her experience – Christ commissioned her to do this before he ascended to the Father (Jn 20:17). We do not know what transformative experiences may have happened to some of the disciples from the witness of Mary. But we hear that the disciples are locked in a room and are fearful of the Jews (Jn 20:19). For the disciples, their fear was the very real threat of their lives being in danger for being followers of Jesus. What we do know of the disciples is that the witness of Mary was not enough; they were still in their spiritual darkness, locked in a room.

Somehow, Jesus appears in the room, giving the disciples peace (Jn 20:19). They witness the risen Lord, and they are filled with joy and gifted with the Holy Spirit (Jn 20:21). After this transformative experience of the risen Lord, there is no more fear and no more darkness. The disciples have complete trust and faith in God. Their faith and spiritual light eventually lead them to death, some more painful and gruesome than others, but they no longer show fear when faced with death. This is how much faith can transform us over time, where we no longer fear being locked in that room in darkness, but are focused on the light. How many of us have felt locked in a room and scared? We can be scared of so many things in life, some can be minor and others more profound. We often use terms such as taking a leap of faith. For example, starting a new job, or a new school. There can be paralysing fear before taking that leap of faith, where we are locked in that room in darkness.

Thomas misses this first encounter and does not believe the other disciples' testimony unless he is able to touch the wounds of Jesus himself. He states that he will not believe (Jn 20:25). I have always wondered why Thomas was so set on not believing the other disciples.

Putting aside the completely extraordinary claim that Jesus had risen, these are the disciples that Thomas had lived with throughout the journey of Jesus' ministry. He knew them, he ate with them, he travelled with them. They told him that their Rabbouni had risen, the one Thomas had listened to and been transformed by throughout his journey with Jesus. What made him not be able to believe unless he could touch the wounds himself? It is a question worth asking, especially in today's world.

Thomas' request was completely unreasonable as proof for the disciples' claims. How often are women or Aboriginal people's experiences not listened to or not believed? We live in a world that is so ready to tell people how they are feeling and what they are experiencing rather than listening to *their* experience and *their* feelings. So many times throughout life, as both an Aboriginal person and as a woman, I have felt that the demands put upon me to prove my experiences were completely unreasonable.

What we don't know is what Thomas went through during that week before he too saw the risen Christ. Maybe he had been moved toward believing. Maybe his fear had decreased. Maybe Christ left his return to Thomas until Thomas was ready for the truth. Christ appeared to the disciples again but this time with Thomas in the room (Jn 20:26). He gave him the opportunity to put his hands in his wounds, but Thomas replied with 'My Lord and my God'. Thomas finally understood – he had his transformative moment from spiritual darkness to light.

Another way we could see this is as Mary preparing the way for the disciples' encounter, and the disciples preparing the way for Thomas' encounter. Just as we saw John the Baptist preparing the way for Jesus (John 3:25–30), others throughout history since the resurrection prepare others for their transformative encounter with Christ in faith.

As a minority person within the Church, both as an Aboriginal and as a woman, it is my task to take this story seriously. There can be great benefits when you are from a minority group. We see things differently, we experience things differently. It means that we constantly see and experience things the way both the majority people and the minority people do. This puts us in a unique position of being capable of a variety of views. I could be like the disciples and be paralysed by fear, locked in a room – or I can be a voice of difference within the Church. It is not easy, and we have come a long way as women but we have a long way to go. We need to be reminded that we should be patient, just as Christ is patient. It took eight days for Thomas – a follower of Jesus, believer in his teachings and brother to the witnesses – to believe in the risen Christ when he encountered him. We have to keep knocking on the door of the Church, we need to continue to be the face of the risen Christ, looking for that transformative experience where the Church is no longer in fear behind locked doors, but open to a leap of faith in welcoming women's voices at the table.

### NOTE

1. All Biblical references are from the *New Revised Standard Updated Edition (NRSV-UE)*, **2021**.

*THE JOURNEY: ADVENT TO RESURRECTION*
*3rd SUNDAY EASTER*

# Feed My Sheep
## On the Gospel of Provision
## John 21:1–19

BETH DOHERTY

Anyone who knows anything about the resurrection of Jesus will know that the women were the first witnesses to the Paschal mystery upon their discovery of the empty tomb. However, by the end of John's Gospel, our doubting brethren are still trying to make sense of what had taken place. In the Gospel of John 21:1–9, in the story about Jesus and the miraculous catch of fish, the disciples are in a bad space. They're struggling to comprehend how the Messiah they followed, the one who promised salvation, could be killed so violently, and they're trying to make sense of it all.

The story is important, because it is one of accompaniment and provision. Here, they must have been wondering if all of the grace and provision that took place during Jesus' life had finished.

Throughout the gospels, there are many stories about bread and fish, staple foods of the place and time. Food, and the sharing of it, is important in the Bible and more generally to our faith. Indeed, the Eucharistic table is known as the 'source and summit'.

If the gospels were to be written today, if we were to experience God's provision in our own lives, would it manifest in an abundant catch of McDonalds, a kale and quinoa salad, or something to satisfy our keto, Paleo, low-carb, gluten-free, pescatarian diets? Perhaps, but more importantly, we must wonder how provision takes place, and what our role might be in the providing. Are there still ordinary, everyday miracles?

It's unlikely many of us have witnessed a genuine, legitimate miracle. God does not literally rain down manna from heaven, but this doesn't mean God is not cooperating with us in the everyday. God provides through God's people. Stories of the saints such as Mary of the Cross MacKillop are often incredible accounts of those who did much with little.

Being very specific, through our churches and organisations, we provide all manner of things. At Christmas last year in my city, a domestic violence shelter for women called MacKillop House was calling for donations and it was women from around the Archdiocese who provided very specifically for the needs of these women. We don't hear about the provision of sanitary pads and tampons in the gospels but these are needs that must be satisfied, and our collaboration with God, whether we see it this way or not, is required here.

Now, do we always get the memo? Well, clearly, we don't.

God collaborates with us. God made a covenant with us in Christ, and we have to do our part. There is a call and response, and we need to be attentive.

Now, since this is a book with a collection of reflections written by women, it's important that some statistics and facts are front and centre. It is perhaps a well-understood reality that women tend to be more altruistic with provision, they tend to think of others before themselves and really model those Gospel values. In fact, according to the Wall Street Journal, in Bangladesh, Nobel Prize-winner Muhammad Yunus, creator of the micro-credit phenomenon, found that women not only repay loans more often than men, but that when women control the money, their families were more likely to benefit from the income.

But I digress. Here we are talking about Jesus and the miraculous catch of fish, but the connections are significant. The gospel stories demonstrate a God who provides for God's people.

There is also another layer to this when we consider those who do not have food to eat.

There is a wonderful development maxim that is used by organisations that work with the world's poor which goes: 'When you give a person a fish, you feed them for a day. When you teach them how to fish, you feed them for a lifetime.'

This is important when reflecting on this particular scripture, because it demonstrates again the need for partnership, the collaboration between God and humanity, and the necessity of listening to the call of God on each of our hearts to love our neighbour.

In the 1970s, Brazilian Catholic Bishop Dom Helder Camara was quoted thus: 'When I give to the poor, they call me a saint. When I ask why it is they have no food, they call me a communist.'[1]

Dom Helder Camara's questions made people uncomfortable, because he was asking people to follow the most basic commandment, calling the rich oligarchy to account for ignoring the poor. Matthew 25:45 tells us: 'Whenever you did this to one of the least of my sisters or brothers, you did it to me.'

There are political implications to these gospels. There are questions we could ask. The Lord meets his disciples with food, fellowship, and serves them at the seashore. At the last supper, he said: 'Do this in memory of me' and thus instituted the Eucharist: the feeding of people with bread and wine.

We might ask the question though about how many hungry people there are in the world and how we can collaborate with God in this work. Why is it that despite God's provision, people still go hungry, 2000 years after Jesus clearly laid out this blueprint for living?

It is clear in the gospels that God desires for us to have what we need, and that throughout history, most of the great saints have themselves been instruments of God's provision.

In this gospel of provision, John 21:1–19, Jesus' words to Peter: 'feed my sheep' are a clear mandate to us to go and do the same.

Much of this gospel is hard to understand, but, with the context of provision, we can understand exactly what God requires of us.

We show our love for God through feeding, providing, and allowing ourselves to be instruments. We follow Jesus by being a conduit for his abundant love.

The greatest commandment is to love others as we love ourselves. Across the world's religions, the Golden Rule shows us that we should treat others as we would wish to be treated.

Our response is our faith. So many of the miracle stories focus on feeding and healing.

To finish, it's worth sharing the words of the late Rachel Held

Evans, a questioner and a modern-day prophet whose book *Searching for Sunday* beautifully sums up the challenge and gift of what it means to be a follower of Jesus:

> On the days when I am hungry – for community, for peace, for belief – I remember what it was like to feed people Jesus, and for people to feed Jesus to me. And those pieces of memory multiply, like the bread that fed the five thousand, spilling out of their baskets and filling every hollow space. Communion doesn't answer every question, nor does it keep my stomach from rumbling from time to time, but I have found that it is enough.[2]

We each need to do our part, feed our sheep, offer whatever small amount we have, and trust that with our help, God will do the rest.

---

**NOTES**

1. Camara, DH, *Dom Helder Camara: Essential Writings*, Orbis Books, USA, 2009.
2. Evans R, *Searching for Sunday*, Thomas Nelson USA, 2015.

*THE JOURNEY: ADVENT TO RESURRECTION*
*6th SUNDAY EASTER*

# Love and Friendship
## The foundations of human dignity
## John 15:9–17

### DANIELLE ANNE LYNCH

Love and friendship are two important concepts to explore in John 15:9–17. This passage reveals something about who we are, how we relate to others, and who we are in relation to and with God.

The gospel speaks of a God who is love and whom we know through love – *agape* – love in action. In a remarkable book called *All About Love*, bell hooks claims that we assume we should know how to love instinctively, but the way forward is to acknowledge how little we know and how often we see poor models of love.[1] We don't all know what it is to experience unconditional parental love. For many of us, openness to love has caused pain and hurt. We often experience love that is not reciprocated. Yet, we continue to desire to love and be loved.

Love is action, not feeling, despite the common interpretation of love as emotion in our society. We need to and can learn how to love through our actions. We therefore have much more control over love than we might imagine if we think of love as emotion. In other words, we choose to love by the way in which we act. And through these actions, others see who we are. Indeed, John 13:35 has Jesus speaking the words: 'By this everyone will know that you are my disciples, if you have love for one another'. Our actions, our choice to act in a loving way, shows us and others who we are. Moreover, our loving actions are witness to our faith in the God of love.

Where, then, might we look for a model of love? As the Gospel says, 'love one another as I have loved you' (John 15:12). If we are to take Jesus as a model for love, we might look to accounts of how Jesus is reported to have acted in relation to his friends and others. We could spend a lifetime studying these accounts – some do! – but if there is an overarching theme in the Gospel accounts which summarises the way in which Jesus acts, for me it is that Jesus' actions affirm the innate dignity of each person he encounters. Therefore, if we are to take seriously the demand to 'love one another', our actions must uphold the dignity of others.

Friendship appears in this Gospel as a relational concept. We create and sustain friendships with others and with Jesus, and, by extension, the Father. We remain in Jesus' love in much the same way as we are surrounded by love when we are encapsulated in an authentic friendship. We can conceptualise our relationship with God as friendship rather than as parent-child relationship. This changes the dynamic of the relationship. Friendship is complex, intricate, ever-changing. It is a mutual relationship chosen between independent people. Friendship is open, trusting, vulnerable.

What does love look like within the realm of friendship? The gift of one's whole self to the other is the greatest love. The trust and vulnerability required of us in authentic friendship is a gift of the self to the other through which the greatest love can be glimpsed. On this, hooks writes, 'To be loving we willingly hear each other's truth and, most importantly, we affirm the value of truth telling.'[2] Only in being truthful to ourselves and others can we enter into meaningful relationships. Love based in truth is fulfilling because we are loved just as we are, for who we are. The gift of the whole self in loving friendship offers a glimpse of God who is love, revealed to us in the sacramental gifts of love and friendship. This is not faith beyond doubt, but faith amidst doubt, as we know and have seen how often and how easily such gifts can be rejected or abused.

Our society teaches us to measure our love, to confine it to certain individuals, to jealously guard love. Yet there is no single way to love. Our loves can interweave, overlap. They are as complex, fluid and unpredictable as everything else in life. To be loving at the cost of self is counter-cultural: societal expectations are that our actions will benefit ourselves. But love in action is other-focused, not self-focused. This was radical at the time of Jesus, as evidenced by the outrage of those around him at his actions, and it remains radical today. This model of radical love empowers us to act in the interest of the dignity and welfare of humans and the world. Yet, it is in the radical act of loving that joy is to be found. Mary Oliver asks at the end of her poem 'The Summer Day': '... what is it you plan to do with your one wild and precious life?' If our response to this was 'I plan to love and be loved', would we be content? Would we be fulfilled? Would our lives have meaning? Would we know ourselves, others, and God?

What is most radical about love based on affirming the innate dignity of others is that it erases the cultural boundaries and barriers that we have created. It is radical because it rejects the principles of a patriarchal society which tell us how and who we can love. It values the love of friendship over romantic love, which is unusual in the dominant discourses of our world today. Indeed, it suggests that all love is based primarily on friendship and that friendship teaches us how to love intimately. Love is beyond categories; it is what makes us human. In loving another, we allow them to be who they are, and love them for that. We say to them, in our words and, more importantly, in our actions, you are enough, you are good, you are beautiful, just as you are. It is in the deep connections formed through vulnerability and trust that there is fulfilment. We witness the presence of the God of love in our own love.

I conclude with the words of a song I wrote as a recontextualisation of the *Lord's Prayer*. It is an example of bringing the Christian faith tradition into dialogue with the contemporary context. This prayer that Jesus taught the first disciples is one way in which Christians follow Jesus' example to love God and others. This prayer of communion excludes no one. It is a call to live our lives in love, in the presence of the God of love, ever in our midst. Through our love, let us all remain in God's love. Pray with me ...

**Into Silence**

Unknown, unnameable, in our midst.
May music speak your name into silence.

Let us together acknowledge the dignity of all people
each created in your image until the end of time.

When we have more than we need, help us to share with others.
May our faults become gifts of healing.

Let us remember to live in the mystery where we seek wisdom
to live in harmony and recognise ourselves in you.

Unknown, unnameable, in our midst.
May music speak your name into silence.[3]

## NOTES

1. hooks b, *All About Love*, pp 27–8.
2. hooks b, *All About Love*, p 81.
3. *Into Silence*, https://www.youtube/5qZF5sxhHFU

## REFERENCES

hooks b, *All About Love*, Perennial, New York (2000).
Lynch D, *Into Silence*, (2020), accessed 5 December 2022, https://www.youtube/5qZF5sxhHFU

*Tempus B*

**TEMPUS B**
**12th SUNDAY**

# Jesus Calms the Storm
## Mark 4:35–41[1]

### ELIZABETH LEE

The Sydney to Hobart Yacht Race of 1998 was a disastrous event. When the starter's pistol fired at 1 pm on Boxing Day 1998, the skies above Sydney were glistening and blue. But within 48 hours the fleet was decimated by a horrendous storm that left 6 sailors dead, 24 yachts abandoned at sea or written off and fewer than half of the 115 starters making it to Hobart.[2]

John 'Steamer' Stanley, a crew member of the *Winston Churchill*, recounted his ordeal:

> We had a sea that just came out of nowhere ... I could feel it from where I was in the aft coach house. It just picked the boat up and then rolled it down its face – 25-tonne of boat – into the trough at a 45-degree angle. It was like hitting a brick wall when we got to the bottom ... Stanley was pinned to the windward side of the coach house and the three windows were smashed. He heard other crew members calling for help up on deck and rushed to find (two of them) hanging in the rigging and around the boom with their feet about two feet off the deck.[3]

Another crew member on the same yacht, Bruce Gould, said:

> ... we were running in these huge seas with the wind over one quarter, getting lower and lower in the water ... Next thing a massive wave, 40 feet plus, came and swamped us. It filled the boat. I said to Richard, 'Well mate, this is it. You'd better tell the boys we're abandoning ship.'[4]

Indeed a ferocious storm, terrifying these experienced crew members.

In Mark 4:35–41, we encounter an equally experienced boating crew who were just as terrified by a storm battering their boat on the Sea of Galilee. For those who have grown up in the Christian tradition, this Gospel story, frequently called 'Jesus calms the storm', is very familiar. We may have become a bit blasé, forgetting how frightening the experience would have been. After all, these disciples were experienced fishermen, well used to encountering storms on the lake. Yet, they were truly frightened, crying out, 'do you not care, we are going down?' (v.39). No doubt they experienced the same fear experienced by the crew of the 1998 Sydney to Hobart yachts. But is the story just about some fishermen caught in a storm and fearful of drowning some 2000 years ago?

The story is placed in Mark's Gospel after Jesus has been preaching about the *Kin-dom* of God. It is the first in a collection of miracle stories and the first of the 'nature' miracles. At the time of writing, the early Christian community was suffering persecution. On hearing the story, they would be reminded of the various passages in the Hebrew scriptures in which God had power over the seas. These include the creation story in Genesis 1, the story of Noah and the flood, the parting of the Red Sea and the story of Jonah, as well as Psalms 65 and 107. This story demonstrates that Jesus has this same Divine power over nature. The stories that follow in the Gospel of Mark go on to demonstrate the power Jesus has over demons, disease and death. The writer of the Gospel is showing Jesus restoring things to the way God intended. To this early Christian community, living amid these storms, it may have seemed that God was silent. Was Mark reminding them not to be afraid, whatever the circumstances, as Jesus is always present?

Likewise, for us, there is an invitation to reflect on how God is present in those times in our lives when everything seems to be going against us and we are being swamped with the beating waves and howling winds of life that are threatening to drown us. Who do we call on in these times? Maybe a family member, a friend, a work colleague or a counsellor? Is the Divine Presence present to us, through this person, amid our storms? Maybe the actual storm is the movement of Divine grace in our lives, such that the experience changes us – becoming more courageous, more trusting, more empathetic. If God's Divine Presence is in all things, then God is present in the storm.

Maybe the storms alert us to the sense that God is silent, just as Jesus was asleep. Silence does not necessarily mean absence.

There is a puzzling line in this story. Having been woken from his sleep by the petrified disciples and having rebuked the wind and calmed the sea, Jesus says to his disciples 'why are you so frightened? How is it that you have no faith?' (v.40). But did not the disciples demonstrate their faith by waking Jesus from his sleep, knowing that he could do something about the storm that was swamping them? That sounds like faith in his miraculous powers. However, maybe there is more. Perhaps the invitation is not to call out to Jesus, to God, to rescue us when our lives are in turmoil and we feel we are drowning. Maybe, our faith is to know that God is with us through the storms and that no matter what the external conditions are, all will be well! We cannot expect to have all the storms quelled as we cry from the depths of the stormy sea any more than the crew of the Sydney to Hobart yachts could expect their cries to suddenly make the wind drop and the seas be calm. But faith does invite us to weather the storms of life, knowing and trusting that somewhere God is present, and we too will look back in awe. Hans Küng (1928–2021) Swiss Catholic priest, theologian, and author is reported to have said, 'God's love does not protect us from suffering. God's love protects us in the midst of suffering'.[5]

We need to remember the context in which this Gospel was written, and that the writer of Mark's Gospel was not offering the story just to individuals but to the early Christian community. Pope Francis warns us of the illusion of individualism.[6] While this Gospel story was addressed to the early Christian community who were living in a chaotic world of persecution, trauma and ongoing disasters, we, too, are living amid a myriad of traumas and disasters, some highly visible, others not so. The invitation is to reflect upon Mark 4:35–41 not only in the storms of our own lives but also in the storms that we are experiencing, locally, nationally, internationally. The early Christian community, like us, were seeking order amid the chaos.

Where is our faith amid the chaos? What are our expectations of God, of the Universal Christ, of one another and of ourselves concerning yet another Black death in custody, continuing imprisonment of asylum seekers, widespread sexual assault and domestic violence or the consequences of climate change? Where is Divine Presence present in these storms?

We will never know if the story is literally true. Does that matter? Instead, how does this story resonate? How are we being invited to live, individually and communally? What will be different because of your encounter with this sacred text? Has your thinking been confirmed, or have you been invited to new ways of seeing? Can you view this story and the stories of others caught up in ferocious storms with fresh eyes? Each time we hear a sacred text, be it from ancient canons or contemporary poets, Gospel writers or news journalists, we are invited to reflect on what the Divine invitation is for me now, to us now?

And then to act, even amid the ferocious storms.

## NOTES

1. *Jerusalem Bible/St Pauls Sunday Missal*, St Pauls, Strathfield, (2012).
2. ABC (Australian Broadcasting Corporation) 'Sydney to Hobart 1998 tragedy 20 years on — the east coast low that changed marine forecasting', ABC News (2018), accessed 24 August 2022.
3. Mundle R, *Fatal Storm: the 54th Sydney to Hobart Yacht Race*, Harper Collins, Pymble, (1999), p 161.
4. *ibid.,* p 164.
5. Küng K, A–Z Quotes, https://www.azquotes.com/quote/1397385, accessed 26 August 2022.
6. CNA (Catholic News Agency), 'Pope Francis warns Catholics that individualism is 'illusory'', CAN News, https://www.catholicnewsagency.com/news/44923/pope-francis-warns-catholics-that-individualism-is-illusory; accessed 24 August 2022.

**TEMPUS B**
**13th SUNDAY**

# Jesus Invites a Woman to Preach
## Mark 5:21–43

### PATRICIA GEMMELL

The cure of the woman with a haemorrhage is told within the story of the raising to life of Jairus' daughter. It is worth mentioning that this gospel is often read in church in its shorter version, with the older woman's story omitted. When we do this, we effectively silence her voice.

There could hardly be a stronger contrast than that between Jairus, a leader of the synagogue, and the unnamed woman suffering a haemorrhage. He is rich, powerful, a man of influence respected by society, who has no hesitation speaking to Jesus to beg for his help. She, on the other hand, is destitute, diseased, voiceless, shunned by society, and too ashamed to approach Jesus other than to touch his tunic from behind. At the moment she touches him, Jesus is already on an emergency mission, hastening to save the life of a little girl at the point of death. But he stops and turns. How must Jairus have felt when he saw that woman come forward and take all of Jesus' attention? She came slowly, reluctantly, in fear and trembling, fell before him, and, according to Mark, told Jesus the whole truth.

Sit with these words. She told him the whole truth. There is a world of meaning and so much to be pondered in these few words.

If we think back to Chapter 1 of Mark's Gospel, when Jesus first taught in the synagogue, we will remember that they were amazed at his teaching because he taught them with authority. Here, in front of the jostling crowds and in front of one of the leaders of the synagogue, Jesus gives this unnamed woman authority to teach. He invites this woman to tell the good news to those around him, in her own words.

He invites her, surely, does he not, to preach to the assembly? I see a leader of the synagogue presiding, in the presence of Jesus and a crowd of his followers. It looks like church to me.

Mark leaves it to us to imagine what she might have said.

There is no doubt that we see in this story Jesus' preferential option for the poor. This apparently worthless woman is worth saving. What is less obvious is the fact that Jesus gives this woman a voice in the assembly, a voice that evangelises her first listeners, but is also meant to evangelise us. She does so with the whole truth of her story.

Maybe Jesus too was changed in that encounter with her strong faith. After she speaks, he addresses her as 'daughter' – what love and tenderness she must have called forth in him! He commends her faith and sends her home in peace.

What did Jairus, distraught about his own daughter, see, hear, and feel, in that moment when Jesus addressed this unknown woman as his daughter? I wonder how Jairus might have been changed that day. Did he see things in a new way? Was his heart expanded?

How would our church be changed if our leaders stopped and listened to the truth of women's stories? How much would the voice of women in the assembly enrich our understanding of God's saving power?

Reflecting on everything that happened after the event, Jairus would have realised that he lost nothing in having to stop for Jesus to heal that woman and restore her to life. It would not have seemed so at the time. What did he learn about his God that day?

For us who would be followers of Jesus of Nazareth, what can we learn of Jesus from the events of that day? Observe him closely. Look at the crowd jostling him, the disciples near him, the man who is confident that Jesus will save his daughter's life, and the woman who knows that all she has to do is touch his tunic and she will be cured. Jesus is hurrying to his destination, the crowds are noisy and excited and jostling him on all sides, and yet he stops and asks, 'Who touched my clothes?' To me, this moment always feels like a freeze frame in a movie.

I can feel the stillness in Jesus, his equanimity, his complete and utter presence in this moment. I fall in love with this Jesus every time. There is about him a truly breath-taking centredness. He knows exactly what he is about. It is as if everything in the whole world stopped for Jesus in that moment when he knew that power had gone out from him. There was absolutely no doubt in his mind that in this moment this was where he was needed. Jairus would have to wait, and in the waiting, he would learn of God's love for all God's people, no matter their gender, wealth or social standing.

This Jesus is more than a miracle worker. He is one with God, totally in tune with God's love for struggling humanity. Only a deeply contemplative Jesus can be this calm and this sensitive in this noisy, distracted, tense situation. We know of Jesus' prayer life because Mark tells us often that Jesus withdrew to lonely places to pray. This is what makes him so responsive to the priorities of any present moment, so quickly able to discern the right path of action in the face of conflicting needs. In this story, he knows that this unnamed woman, whose sickness is now cured, is still in need of healing. He gives her the opportunity to be seen and heard for who she is, to be known, not judged but accepted. Telling her story is ultimately what heals her.

In listening to her story, we are evangelised. We hear the good news: Jesus is our Saviour and the kingdom of God has drawn near, but we also hear that it is ultimately our faith that will save us.

When Jairus was told that his daughter had died and there was no longer any need for help, Jesus said to him, 'Do not fear. Only believe, and she will be saved.' Jairus did have faith and his daughter was restored to him. But I wonder. Would he have found that faith within him if he hadn't first witnessed the faith of the woman with the haemorrhage and seen what Jesus had been able to do for her? It is quite possible that she deepened the faith Jairus already had. If she could do that to him, can she still now do it to us? We only need to imagine her voice in our ears and take care how we listen.

Mark knew the power of truth-telling in story. He wrote his gospel for a suffering community in deeply troubled times. He wanted to demonstrate that God is always with us, ready to save, ready to bring us back to life. All we need is to have faith. But faith comes from hearing the stories. In our own troubled times, we need to hear as many voices of faith as possible.

What is the invitation in this gospel? For me, it is to have the courage to raise my voice in the assembly and tell my truth. It is to learn to pray as Jesus did. What is it for you?

---

QUESTIONS FOR REFLECTION

- What do you imagine was the 'whole truth' as told by the woman?
- What does this story say to you about the nature of faith?
- What is the invitation to you in this gospel?

**TEMPUS B**
**21st SUNDAY**

# Enough Bread Talk – I'm Outta Here!
## John 6:60–69

### CATHIE LAMBERT

I wonder if you have ever played the community-building game where someone begins a story with a sentence or two and it is then passed to the next person to add their contribution. The story continues from person to person, gaining momentum and hilarity as it progresses. It is an activity I recall around campfires, at youth group events, at large family gatherings, and with young people for whom English is a second language. It is a simple game, with few rules and can involve people of all ages and abilities. It is a great icebreaker, an effective time-filler and, often, a seriously good laugh. There is, however, one essential element in this game – participation. At times people in the circle fail to contribute, pass to the next person or spend too long thinking. As a result, the story falters, the laughter fades, the game falls flat. Participation is the key, but you have no idea where the story will head next or any clue what your next contribution will be until the story lands in your lap.

In John 6:60–69, we come to the end of what has seemed a long string of bread stories which have perhaps become a little monotonous compared to the game just described. And so, we come to this odd encounter to conclude the chapter. A group of disciples choose to turn back and no longer follow Jesus. These are not 'church shoppers' stopping by to try Jesus out; these are disciples, those committed to following Jesus' way. So, what is it that causes them to leave? Is it simply that they have had enough of the bread talk? Or is there something more?

The text suggests that what Jesus is teaching is simply too hard for these people. Perhaps, this was not the Christ they had hoped for. Like many today, maybe they wanted a saviour with a magic wand who would fix the problems of the world. Instead, Jesus is asking for full participation from his disciples. His talk of bread ends with Jesus suggesting he is the bread of life – and they must eat.

Of course, a literal, physical understanding completely misses Jesus' point. Jesus drew crowds wherever he travelled. People would come and listen to his teaching or would stand by in hope of healing. Here though, Jesus is saying 'Don't just stand by waiting for some miracle: devour my teaching, let it become part of you, so that you too are transformed and become part of this life-giving movement'. Jesus is seeking a 'yes' to the life he offers, a commitment which requires getting involved.

Richard Rohr talks about two types of faith.[1] He calls them positive faith and negative faith. I like to think of them more as 'Yes' faith and 'No' faith. Rohr argues it is much easier to gather people around a 'No' faith. People who want to say no to abortion, or ill-treatment of refugees, or violence against women, or marriage equality. Whatever the issue may be, if people want to say no, there is a lot of energy and crowds will gather. It is much more difficult to gather people to say 'yes' to something. A 'yes' faith is intimate. It is not about what you are fighting or what you are against; but instead focuses on the thing you are in love with, the thing you desire, that which gets you out of bed each morning. What is that for you?

In John 6:60–69, we see these two played out. The disciples who turned away followed Jesus in the hope that he would have the answers to changing the world around them. Perhaps, they and the crowds gathered with a 'no' to Roman domination, a 'no' to the injustices they were experiencing, a 'no' to corruption and hypocrisy. In hearing Jesus' teaching, the fear that drives them kicks in. Perhaps it is the fear of losing their tradition, their family, their life. Jesus is asking too much in asking them to say 'yes'. And then Jesus turns to the twelve, 'Do you also wish to go away?' (v.67). Although Peter often stumbles and fumbles his way through life, here he answers with a 'yes'. 'Lord, to whom can we go? You have the words of eternal life' (v.68). These are the words of someone who has experienced the Divine love offered and can see no other way.

I cannot help but relate this passage to my research with women who find themselves on the edge of the church.[2] In today's society, with declining church attendance and aging congregations, this passage could be used by church goers to justify their pious position and throw judgment at those who have chosen to leave the institutional church. I have been heavily involved in church throughout my life. It has been an important foundation for my faith. But I must say, I have seen an awful lot of people come along very passively, ready to sit and soak up whatever the person at the front has to offer. Is attending church about saying 'yes' to God or following Jesus? Many of the women I interviewed in my research no longer attend church. Some may say they have lost their way, or have regressed. In listening to their stories, however, it is evident that for many of them their choice was to move away from a 'no' faith towards a 'yes' faith. Their choice to participate more fully in God's story led them out into the community and to deep places in their relationship with God. The passage from John is not about loyalty, it is about participation.

The historical women I introduced to these contemporary women on the edge of the church knew about this full participation. The beguine mystics from the thirteenth century speak of their relationship with God with great intimacy. Mechthild of Magdeburg, in Book 4 of her *Flowing Light of the Godhead*, says:

> God has enough
> Of all good things
> Except one:
> Of communion with humans
> God can never have enough.[3]

This is the reason Mechthild got up every morning – to commune with her God, to fully participate in her relationship with the Divine. This 'yes' to relationship with God is not passive. It bubbles over in acts of service, cries for justice, advocacy, feeding the hungry, sitting with those in prison, and maybe in attending church. This 'yes' cannot be contained or controlled. It can be scary. It can involve risk.

This 'yes' that Jesus is calling for from his disciples is about God's love becoming one with our lives. Just as the bread we consume becomes part of our body, our very being, so too does the love of God. No longer can we compartmentalise our lives into different containers, restricting our spiritual lives to one day of the week. There is no longer any distinction between secular and sacred when we fully participate in our relationship with God. A short passage from Kahlil Gibran's *The Prophet*[4] poetically makes this point. It uses the bread imagery of John 6. I have changed the words slightly to make them inclusive.

### The Prophet

…Like sheaves of corn [God] gathers you unto [Godself].
[God] threshes you to make you naked.
[God] sifts you to free you from your husks.
[God] grinds you to whiteness.
[God] kneads you until you are pliant;
And then [God] assigns you to [God's] sacred fire, that you may become sacred bread for God's sacred feast.

All these things shall love do unto you that you may know the secrets of your heart, and in that knowledge become a fragment of Life's heart…

When you love you should not say,
'God is in my heart,' but rather,
'I am in the heart of God.'

May your 'yes', to being in the heart of God, bless you this day. Amen.

---

### NOTES

1. Rohr R, 'What You Wake Up for in the Morning' [video], Centre for Action and Contemplation, Facebook Video, 23 August 2015, accessed 9 July 2021.
2. Lambert C, 'Dwelling on the Edge: A Spiritual Director Hears Contemporary Women Respond to the Beguine Mystics' [unpublished PhD thesis], University of Divinity, 2022.
3. Mechthild of Magdeburg, *The Flowing Light of the Godhead* (F Tobin trans), Paulist Press, Mahwah, NJ, 1998, p 153.
4. Gibran K, *The Prophet*, accessed at Gutenberg https://www.gutenberg.org/files/58585/58585-h/58585-h.htm on 8 December 2022.

*TEMPUS B*
*23rd SUNDAY*

# Be Opened
## Mark 7:31–37

### FIONA DYBALL

Leading New Testament scholar Dan Harrington SJ names Jesus as the model for the Markan church: a church on mission that 'goes beyond the bounds of its own culture and joins the proclamation of the gospel to the active ministry of confronting human suffering'.[1] This earliest, shortest, and most vivid gospel book comes to life with details and human touches that make it both attractive and often quite disturbing. There's an immediacy in the storytelling that readily allows people to imagine themselves as part of the action. While this can be confronting, it is also freeing and consistently grounding.

This story is not found in any other gospel. It tells of Jesus healing a Gentile man who is deaf and who also has an impediment in his speech. At this time in history, being deaf and unable to speak clearly would probably have been isolating and lonely, as illness and disability could be seen as being caused by demonic possession or divine punishment. Jesus chooses to enter into the man's suffering and stand with him, drawing close rather than keeping his distance. Australian New Testament scholar Brendan Byrne SJ describes this healing by Jesus as restoring the hearing and speaking world of interpersonal communication to the man and restoring his place and life in community.[2]

Jesus takes the man away from the crowd, touches his ears and anoints his tongue, groaning to heaven so that hearing and speech may 'be opened' for the man. The Aramaic word for this opening, Ephphatha, is preserved in the original text, and – significantly – in the modern Rite of Baptism.[3] Although there were many fake faith healers at this time, Jesus offers power far beyond magic words, mere spectacle, and empty promises. Jesus' integrated words and actions visibly renew life. The story shows the compassionate power of God at work in surprisingly personal and tender encounters. People's lives open up when they can give and receive, understand, and be understood.

Jesus' ministry here is characterised by physical presence and proximity that both announce and enact the reign of God. Theologian M. Shawn Copeland, in her book *Knowing Christ Crucified: The Witness of African American Religious Experience* observes that Jesus consistently places his body directly with the bodies of people who are poor, excluded, or despised by mainstream society or powerful rulers.[4] The incarnation is forever joined with social justice, with life poured out for and with others. Worship anchors this outwardly focused eucharistic living as the Body of Christ in action in the world. Jesus gives people the gift of himself, and healing involves both individual and communal dimensions of liberation.

There's no doubt that these are anything but ordinary times. Despite being connected by technology like never before, the COVID-19 pandemic has still resulted in many people feeling closed in and off over these past few years. Recently we have been less able to gather together in person to work and socialise, to share activities like sport and the arts that build wellbeing and belonging, and to freely celebrate or grieve together in large numbers. Zoom and other online meeting options are valuable and helpful but there is a clear recognition that being together in a more embodied way is different. Jesus' invitation is to a deeper understanding of freedom in discipleship through these times. The Spirit opens ways for healing in any situation if we are open to it working in us; this opening may appear where and how we least expect it. In exploring practical and symbolic interpretations of this Gospel, it helps me to imagine each character as offering a different invitation to openness.

The people who brought their friend to Jesus to be healed cared enough to do it. As St Mary MacKillop so often said, 'Never see a need without doing something about it.'[5] Openness to walking with a person struggling, and seeking additional support for them when needed, is the heart of advocacy. Faithfully playing our part in accompanying people over time can help them to find their own voice. This happens in a range of ways: regular conversations, practical help, sharing a sacrament, or connecting to specialist groups and services. Friendship is often what people crave most of all. In opening to what can be done, there's a step taken towards something better for someone who may not be able to find a way forward on their own at this point in their life.

The person brought to Jesus was unable to hear, or to speak so that they could be understood. In order to respond to the Gospel, we have to be able to hear it. Are we people of hope, open to receiving God's love in the goodness available to us right now? Are we closed to the cry of the earth and the cry of the poor, locked in a self-centredness or fear that make us deaf to those who need time, resources, and care? Does our silence give permission for harm to other people, creatures, and the earth to continue because we're more concerned with comfort, profit, or professional and social standing? Mary Oliver in her insightful poem 'Sometimes' gives three instructions for living a life: 'Pay attention. Be astonished. Tell about it.'[6] As Christians, we are called to open our hearts and minds to pay attention to both the joys and the struggles faced by ourselves and others. We are called to open our ears and eyes to be astonished by both the beauty and the horror present in our world. And we are called to open our lips in praise for the amazing grace that surrounds us, and to lament injustices, speaking the truth in love so that lasting change can come.

The last invitation in our Gospel today comes from Jesus. The simplicity and earthiness of Jesus' words and actions are disarming, and instructive. There's no judgment of the person suffering by Jesus, no blaming or shaming, no publicity sought, no debt to pay. Jesus compassionately and freely opens an integrated wholeness in the person, reconnecting them to their community. Faith, hope, and love come together in relationship: the faith of the advocates seeking new life for their friend; the hope of the person who turns to Jesus in their need; and in the love of God constantly at work within us and in our world – even in a pandemic. God invites us to participate as disciples in the here and now by healing physical, mental, and spiritual wounds as we can. We open inclusive spaces and ways for all people to belong so that they can hear the music of their own lives rising within them and give voice to their own unique song. Their voice can then join the harmony of the community chorus that lifts us all.

Music plays a key role in the way I express my life in community. It shapes my identity and prayer in relationship with the living God: central to this is the ability to be open, to listen, and to respond. It is also central to our Gospel today. By baptism, we are opened to the music of God's Spirit moving in us and guiding us in our lives. In our shared song, we stand in solidarity together across time and space. The God of both the singer and the song is always with us.

From the hymn 'God's Call':
Let love and peace be born in me. Do not be afraid!
Trust in the mystery of God's Life.
Be born in us today. Jesus, you are The Way.

## NOTES

1. Harrington, *Sacra Pagina: Mark*, 242.
2. Byrne, *A Costly Freedom*, 126–127.
3. 'Catholic Rite of Baptism for Children', Article 31, 3; RCIA (1986), Ephphetha Rite, Articles 184–187.
4. Copeland, *Knowing Christ Crucified*, (1987), 83.
5. MacKillop, M, accessed at MacKillop Family Services, https://www.mackillop.org.au/news/mackillop-annual-public-meeting-2019 accessed on 8 December 2022.
6. Oliver, M, *Devotions: The Selected Poems of Mary Oliver*, Penguin Press, New York, (2017).

## REFERENCES

Byrne B SJ, *A Costly Freedom: A Theological Reading of Mark's Gospel*, Liturgical Press, Collegeville, 2008.
Copeland MS, *Knowing Christ Crucified: The Witness of African American Religious Experience*, Fortress Press, Minneapolis, 2018.
Harrington D SJ (ed), *Sacra Pagina: The Gospel of Mark*, Liturgical Press, Collegeville, 2002.
MacKillop Family Services, https://www.mackillop.org.au/news/mackillop-annual-public-meeting-2019 accessed on 8 December 2022.
Oliver M, *Devotions: The Selected Poems of Mary Oliver*, Penguin Press, New York, 2017.

**TEMPUS B
27th SUNDAY**

# Original Love
## Mark 10:2–16

### MARY COLOE

The Gospel for the 27th Sunday of the Year B, is Mark 10:2–16, the famous passage on divorce. Jesus' teaching in this passage is radical. It goes against the social customs in the Jewish world of his time, and even the Law of Moses.

In western societies today, women as well as men can instigate divorce – even though, unless the woman has independent wealth and power, she usually comes off second best. In Judea during the first century CE, only the man could divorce his wife and that could be because the marriage bore no children (which was always considered to be caused by the woman's infertility) or the woman in some other way displeased her husband.

The divorce happened simply by the husband stating before witnesses that he was divorcing his wife and then, according to the law in Deuteronomy 24:1–4, he gave her in writing a statement of divorce, making it possible for her to remarry.

If a woman was divorced, she left her husband's house with only her dowry, which was usually the clothes and other jewellery or coins that she was wearing. She then had to return to her father's house to live under his authority, or the authority of the eldest son, until he could find another husband for her. If there were any children of the marriage, they stayed with the father and she had no claim on them. In this situation, a woman had no redress: she could not divorce her husband for any reason. Clearly, by social custom and law, the woman was left in a vulnerable and powerless situation, with no rights and little prospect of a future marriage.

In Mark 10:2 when the Pharisees ask, 'Is it lawful for a man to divorce his wife?' they are not asking out of concern about the law: it is a trick question to test Jesus. Up until this point, Jesus had been in the northern region of Galilee and his teaching and healings included women (Mark 1:29–31; 5:34, 41); he referred to his followers as his kin, his 'brothers and sisters and mother' (3:35). Even when he travelled into Gentile territory his healing included the daughter of a Syrophoenician woman (7:29), followed by feeding a crowd of Gentile women and men (8:9). According to strict Jewish expectations he had not followed the pattern of a Jewish rabbi. This question about divorce was to test his credibility, particularly his attitude to women, which up till now had been quite scandalous.

The Pharisees were lay teachers of the law and in reply to their test, Mark depicts Jesus using their own Scriptures against them; he gives them a lesson in biblical interpretation. He points to a teaching even earlier than the man-made law of Moses that they recall (10:4); he speaks of God's initial act of creation when man and woman were made together in Genesis 1:27.

Jesus interprets (10:5) the later law of Moses as a response to the Israelites' 'hardness of heart' in the wilderness, an expression that links their attitude with that of the Pharaoh of Egypt, whose 'hardness of heart' kept the children of Israel enslaved in Egypt (Exod 7:3, 22; 8:15).

Things are not looking good for the Pharisees. They have come up against a man, seemingly with no formal education, but one who knows the Torah and is now using it to relook at God's original desire for men and women.

Jesus first quotes Genesis 1: 'God made them male and female'. Because he is speaking to learned men there is no need to quote the entire verse: 'So God created humankind in his image, in the image of God he created them; male and female he created them' (Gen 1:27). This verse, at the beginning of Israel's Torah, affirms that women and men are created equally as bearers of the divine image. This teaching deconstructs the tradition of patriarchy that would give a man rights over a woman, and allow a man to cast aside his wife through divorce.

But Jesus has not finished his scripture lesson with the Pharisees.

He then moves to the teaching in Genesis 2, which uses a different tradition to speak about creation, and describes the creation of a man and a woman with these words:

'And the rib that the Lord God had taken from the Adam (the earthling) God made into a woman and brought her to the earthling. [Genesis here is playing on the Hebrew word for 'earth' which is *Adamah*, and the creature made from the earth called *adam* – 'earthling', from earth]. The earthling cried out – "Here at last is bone of my bone and flesh of my flesh; she shall be called woman, for she was taken out of man." Therefore, a man leaves his father and his mother and clings to his wife, and they become one flesh' (Gen 2:22–23). (*Own translation.*)

Notice this great song of delight, and song of recognition. Here there is equality of being. No patriarchy. Genesis 2 describes the world as God desires it to be with harmony between humankind, creation and God. It is God's dream of original love.

But as you know, and the author of this story knew, this dream of God is not the way the world is. So, how can this ancient theologian make sense of the world around him?

He does this by introducing a talking snake in Genesis 3. This serpent, a symbol borrowed from other cultures and myths, tempts the man and the woman to break from God, and to become like God by eating a fruit from a special tree (Gen 3:4). The couple do not realise that they are already made in God's image, and they fall for the serpent's trick. This act of disobedience brings sin and disharmony into the world, and this sinful world is described as patriarchal – 'your desire will be for your husband, and he shall rule over you' (Gen 3:16).

But look where this statement comes! It is not part of God's original desire described in Genesis 2; it is a consequence of sin described in Genesis 3. I find this amazing – that an ancient writer, living in a patriarchal world, has the insight to realise that patriarchy is sinful – it is not of God.

These two Genesis accounts of original creation are brought into Jesus' response to the Pharisees through the quoting of just a few verses. Just a few words allude to the whole passage, and bring the whole passage into the argument, which was a standard way of debating a point of law.

In debating with these Jewish teachers of the Law, Jesus has used teaching from the book of Deuteronomy, made allusions to the book of Exodus, and quoted from Genesis. He has given them a lesson in biblical interpretation. In this way Jesus discounts the later reinterpretation found in Deuteronomy where men were permitted to divorce their wives as a concession to human frailty, to human sinfulness.

Returning to the initial question: Jesus argues against divorce, either instigated by a man (as in Judaism) or by a woman (as Roman Law allowed) as this is not God's original desire for men and women. God's desire was for love, equality, delight, harmony and joy.

Jesus' radical teaching flows from his equally radical vision of the imminent reign of God. In a world where God's desires are no longer thwarted by the power of evil, God's original desire for the loving union of marriage will be realised. In such a world where sin has been vanquished, divorce will have no meaning.

The world of God's desire is called in the gospels – the 'kingdom of God' – where God's dream is realised. I prefer to speak of 'the kindom of God' which emphasises relationship rather than 'power over'. The following verses in Mark (10:13–16), offer insight into this dream: it is a place where children can be at home with their sense of playfulness, trust and the innocent inclusive love of a child.

Can we dare to open ourselves to this dream, in how we reach out to others with hospitality, with kindness, forgiveness, patience – dare I say – with love?

**TEMPUS B**
**32nd SUNDAY**

# Through Jesus' Eyes
## Mark 12:38–44

### MICHELE CONNOLLY

The gospel passage from Mark 12:41–44 depicts Jesus commenting on a widow who gave her last two pennies into the treasury of the temple in Jerusalem. This story has been the basis of many homilies about giving to God or the church even from our poverty, giving to the point of real cost. Such homilies miss the point of this story, which is a homily in itself.

To hear the homily's message, we need to read it attentively and then understand it in the context of the larger gospel narrative in which it occurs.

As the story opens, we notice that Jesus does not interact with this woman in any way; he simply observes her from a bit of a distance. We see her actions through Jesus' eyes, and we overhear the interpretation of her actions that Jesus makes to his disciples. Just like Jesus' disciples, we see the widow as Jesus sees her and we hear what Jesus points out to them.[1]

Mark emphasises that Jesus was sitting opposite the Temple treasury, as he watched how the crowd threw coins into the treasury, with many rich people putting in very much. Sitting opposite the treasury, Jesus has a good view as he watches and gives a judgement on this process.[2] He also no doubt hears the noise of much coin being tumbled into the treasury. There were thirteen trumpet-shaped openings out in the open where people could make contributions to the Temple. Since all money was metal coin, it was no doubt easy to hear if someone contributed a great deal or only a little.

Through the medium of Jesus' intense gaze, we see a poor widow come along, who throws in two small coins, which Mark says is worth a 'quadrant'. The scholars say this was the smallest coin there was, and could buy at most, a scanty meal, enough flour to make a small scone.[3]

Then, calling his disciples to him, Jesus insists with his 'Amen I say to you' expression that the widow has put in more than all the others. This asserts the relative cost each of the donors has endured: the big givers gave from what they had in excess while the poor widow from what she did not have, her actual neediness. Further, Jesus says that she gave 'all she had', which he describes as 'her whole life' (v.44).

Many preachers stop at this point and leave us with the sense that we should give beyond our own need, even to the point of our whole living. Yet, most of us sense that there is something out of proportion here and find the story or its interpretation unsatisfying.

However, if we attend to where Mark has put this story in his gospel, we can see it in a completely different light. What leads up to the story is a long chapter (Mark 12:1–40) where Jesus engages in pointed debate with various leaders of his own religious tradition. Jesus argues that those responsible for this tradition are incompetent, unworthy custodians who do not live by their own rules, do not know the Scriptures or God and hypocritically seek glory, exploiting the weak and above all widows.[4] As a final word, Jesus accuses the scribes, saying that they 'devour widows' houses and for the sake of appearance say long prayers' (v.40).

In the very next verse after Jesus' condemnation of the exploitation of widows, Mark places our story about the widow. So, having just heard about widows' houses being devoured by religious authority figures, we now see just such an example: a poor widow. But there is a following scene, which makes Jesus' remarks even more outstanding. Immediately following the widow's story, Jesus goes out of Jerusalem to the east and sits on the Mount of Olives. There he declares that the huge physical structure of the Temple will be thrown to the ground, with not one stone left upon another (Mark 13:2).

So, within the space of a chapter, Jesus has been depicted declaring the leadership of his own religious tradition to be morally, intellectually and religiously bankrupt – and also, about to be completely destroyed. Yet, it is into this religious tradition that the widow gives all she has to live on, which a person such as herself could well have received from that Temple system, in the form of organised care of the poor, in the first place![5]

Surely the widow's behaviour is crazy, a self-defeating cycle of futility!

However, a final point to remember is that Mark's story of the widow is the last story, the final word of Jesus' public ministry of preaching the gospel. After this story and a special, apocalyptic interlude in Mark 13, the gospel narrative moves into the long Passion Narrative in which Jesus himself will give his 'whole life', will be buried and be raised from the tomb.

Scholars debate whether Jesus commends or laments the widow's act.[6] It is not either / or but a both / and situation. Jesus commends the widow's limitless generosity, prefiguring what he himself will do. And the evangelist Mark places this story of a widow precisely here, to make a final appeal to all of Jesus' disciples. The appeal is this: here is a person who is perfect disciple material, but she is giving her discipleship to the wrong thing![7]

The widow is an embodied appeal, a parable, to Jesus' disciples to proclaim the reign of God to all people, so that they give their lives to the God revealed to us by Jesus, God who will repay with a 100-fold return (Mark 4:1–9).[8] It is the evangelist who places this story at this point, as a final, ironic challenge to all who have witnessed Jesus' public ministry to offer the gift of God's kingdom to people radically in need of it. Presenting the last word of Jesus' public ministry, the story is Mark's dramatic homily to all disciples: go out and offer to people the vision of God Jesus has been proclaiming.

## NOTES

1. Kubiś A, 'The Poor Widow's Mites: A Contextual Reading of Mark 12:41–44', *The Biblical Annal 3, no. 2* (September 2013):343.
2. *Ibid.*, 344.
3. Evans CA, *Mark 8:27–16:20: Word Biblical Commentary*, Nashville: Thomas Nelson, 2001), 282.
4. Fitzmyer JA, *The Acts of the Apostles: A New Translation with Introduction and Commentary*, New York: Doubleday, 1998, 345, cites Old Testament texts that show God's special concern for widows.
5. Strack HL and Billerbeck P, *A Commentary on the New Testament from the Talmud and Midrash Volume 2* (München: C.H.Beck'sche Verlagsbuchhandlung, 1922. Copyright 2022, Lexham Press Volume 2), 50–51 for details on the Temple system of providing for the poor.
6. Wright AG, 'The Widow's Mites: Praise or Lament? – A Matter of Context', *Catholic Biblical Quarterly 44* (1982): 256–65 began this debate.
7. Kozar JV, 'The Owl and the Pussycat: An Off Kilter Reading of the Widow's Honorable Action at the Temple Treasury in Mark 12:41–44', *Proceedings 28* (2008): 46 refers to the widow's 'inchoate example of total giving'.
8. Malbon ES, 'Reflections on Mark 12:38–44 for the Twenty-Fifth Sunday after Pentecost', *Currents in Theology and Mission 44, no. 4* (October 2017): 38 argues that the story operates at a symbolic level as an 'enacted parable'.

## REFERENCES

Evans CA, *Mark 8:27–16:20*, Nashville: Thomas Nelson, 2001.
Fitzmyer JA, *The Acts of the Apostles. A New Translation with Introduction and Commentary*, New York: Doubleday, 1998.
Kozar JV, 'The Owl and the Pussycat: An Off Kilter Reading of the Widow's Honorable Action at the Temple Treasury in Mark 12:41–44', *Proceedings 28*, 2008, pp 41–53.
Kubiś A, 'The Poor Widow's Mites: A Contextual Reading of Mark 12:41–44', *The Biblical Annal 3, no. 2*, September 2013, pp 339–81.
Malbon ES, 'Reflections on Mark 12:38–44 for the Twenty–Fifth Sunday after Pentecost', *Currents in Theology and Mission 44, no. 4*, October 2017, pp 37–42.
Strack HL, Billerbeck P, *A Commentary on the New Testament from the Talmud and Midrash Volume 2*, München: C.H.Beck'sche Verlagsbuchhandlung, 1922. Copyright 2022, Lexham Press Volume 2.
Wright AG, 'The Widow's Mites: Praise or Lament? – A Matter of Context', *Catholic Biblical Quarterly 44*, 1982, pp 256–65.

**TEMPUS B**
**33rd SUNDAY**

# Staying the Course
## Mark 13:24–32

### RADHIKA SUKUMAR-WHITE

It's hard to know what to do with readings like that of Mark Chapter 13, verses 24 to 32. Do we hear them as hyperbole or literal truth? Humanity often reacts to things we find shocking and confronting with hyperbolic language.

In late 2014 when the cricketer Phil Hughes died, my husband and I were in a student ministry placement in the Byron Shire, which was our rural field education placement (#sufferingforthelord…). When the news broke, a lot of that kind of language was used. Perhaps people would have been less shocked if he had died in a car accident; but people struggled with the idea that someone could get killed by playing cricket. And so people resorted to extreme and imaginative language to try to put their shock and confusion into words. The sun refused to shine. The sky has fallen in. The earth has been shaken. Reality has been turned on its head.

We know what is being meant because we are in the middle of the experience. But when we read the apocalyptic language in the Bible, like that of this reading, we are not within the context that produced the words, and we are not sure whether they refer to the landscape of communal emotions or to literal apocalyptic events.

Which brings us to the other difficulty of interpretation, and that is context. Whatever Jesus had actually said, Mark understood them to relate directly to the Roman army destroying the temple in Jerusalem. This actually happened about forty years after the time of Jesus, at about the time that Mark's Gospel was being written. The temple was so central to Judaism that its destruction seemed like the destruction of Judaism and the destruction of the world as they knew it, and so those who were familiar with the apocalyptic statements that Jesus had made naturally understood his words as a foreshadowing of these events that they were now living through.

With that in mind, we could just conclude these apocalyptic passages are of no relevance to us. Or we could conclude that the first-century Christians were wrong because the world didn't end and the Second Coming didn't happen, and therefore what Jesus was pointing to is still ahead of us and maybe coming soon. Or we could conclude that Jesus's words were not tied to a single event, but that he was speaking to both the destroying of the temple and to the fact that these kinds of things keep on happening, and that they always feel like they are the end of the world when you are in the midst of them, but as each one passes, another one arises to terrify us again.

I lean strongly towards that last approach, but it's not enough. Just knowing that Jesus said crazy things will keep happening doesn't give us the comfort and hope we yearn for. So where is Jesus leading us with these apocalyptic warnings, this Advent?

If there's one thing we know about Jesus, it's that he lived what he taught. And the apocalyptic language of the gospel passage for today sounds an awful lot like the events surrounding his own gruesome and violent death – the sky turning dark, suffering among the people, the powers in the heavens being shaken.

So, I wonder if what Jesus reveals in today's teaching and in his experience of violence, is that the only way we have known to control violence is to convince ourselves that there is a difference between good violence and bad violence, and that good violence can be used to control bad violence and prevent it spiralling into apocalypse. Good violence is violence exercised by good people and authorised by a good God for the sole purpose of preventing bad people from using bad violence against good people. This belief and its application have enabled us to contain and control chaos for thousands of years.

But then something went wrong. Suddenly, we all agreed that Jesus was one of the bad people that we had to use our good violence against, and we were all pumping our fists in the street chanting 'Crucify him. Crucify him!' And we crucified him, but he came back, and he was so full of love and grace that we couldn't even pretend to believe that he'd been one of the bad people. And so, the theory fell apart. It became obvious that we weren't very good at telling the difference between good and bad at all: that the truth of the matter was that what we called 'good' violence was really just 'our' violence. And that what we called 'bad' violence was really just 'their' violence. And that actually many of the victims of our 'good' violence were no worse and no more deserving of it than us.

The implications have been sinking in ever since, and what it usually means now is that it is virtually impossible to get a consensus that 'they' are bad and need to be attacked. We still try. Politicians today demonise, say, asylum seekers, and try to get us all to unite against these enemies of...something, but now we keep seeing the humanity of the victims, and we keep hearing the whispered voice of Jesus saying, 'When you do that to one of the least of these, you are doing it to me. In fact, you are doing what you already did to me.'

So now, in the same manner as the drug Thalidomide from the '60s that was said to cure morning sickness but ended up deforming at least 10,000 babies, we recognise that our 'cure' for the whole world is creating more problems than it is solving. Jesus does offer us a new cure, based on universal mutual love and forgiveness, but we are living in a terrifying time lag where the old cure has been exposed, but the new one is a long way from being implemented. Violence, no matter how justified it seems, just goes on breeding more violence and the apocalypse seems closer than ever.

In the face of all this, friends, Jesus doesn't offer any easy answers. He just offers reminders in this reading, and warnings in the next part of the reading. Look at the fig tree; look for signs of new life and hope all around you, hidden in plain sight. Slow right down, and savour little moments of joy in your lives.

And then, 'Keep alert. Stay awake. Be on guard'. Salvation will not come in the form of new improved weapons, or new improved intelligence to ensure that our targeting of evil is more accurate. Salvation will come in the form of an asylum-seeker baby born in a back shed, a baby that the power of Rome will seek to destroy. 'Read the signs', says Jesus, so that you will understand that the innocent victims are all connected, and when you accept any of them as collateral damage, you are accepting that baby in the manger as collateral damage. 'Stay awake' to the temptation to again try to use the force of law and the threat of God's judgement to try to enforce morality and security.

Stay the course that Jesus has begun, for although it is seemingly plunging us into apocalyptic chaos, the plunge is the same as the road to the cross. It is the deeply vulnerable road that goes through suffering and death and beyond and rises into the promised land of life and peace. Stay the course because in the end, the world we yearn for will come, not as an explosion of power and judgement, but as a refugee child, living among the least, dying between two criminals, and rising in solidarity with all the nameless victims of our misguided attempts to destroy evil, rising not in vengeance, but in overwhelming earth-shattering, apocalyptic love and mercy and grace. And for the advent of that day, we work and pray.

Come, Lord Jesus, come. Amen.

*Tempus C*

**TEMPUS C**
**BAPTISM OF THE LORD**

# Part of Who We Are
## Luke 3:15–16, 21–22

### MONICA DUTTON

The gospel of the Baptism of the Lord is read as we move from the infancy narratives of the liturgical season of Christmas and transition to Ordinary Time, during which we engage with the life and mission of the adult Jesus. In Year C it is situated between the Epiphany of the Lord and the Wedding Feast of Cana. These three gospels together proclaim the revelation of Jesus to the world and mark the beginning of his public ministry.

Jesus' baptism by water appears in the three synoptic gospels – those of Matthew, Mark and Luke; while in John's account the emphasis is not on water, but on Jesus receiving the Spirit. While the baptism story offers many entry points for deeper contemplation, the themes of identity and of mission are the focus of this reflection.

The most recent baptism I attended was that of my third grandchild, Ivy Charlotte. Ivy was three months old when she was baptised, and she looked adorable in a beautiful white family christening gown that had been worn by her brother, her mother and many of her aunts, uncles and cousins. Her name was inscribed on a special 'Child of God' Baptismal Candle from Jamberoo Abbey, and it was decorated with delicate pink and white flowers. The other thing about Ivy's baptism was that she had two godmothers (no godfather), and these two doting aunties were referred to throughout the day as her 'fairy godmothers'.

Ivy is blessed with a large family, and due to the COVID-19 restrictions in place at the time, the festivities after the ceremony were held on picnic tables and fold-up chairs under the trees in a local park. It was a wonderful day of family fun and celebration.

Given the current Australian Catholic landscape and the widespread disconnect of millennials from engagement with the rituals and celebrations of the Church, I was somewhat intrigued as to why Ivy's parents (my son and his wife) had decided to have her baptised. My son's simple reply to this question was 'at the end of the day it's part of who we are'.

I was struck by the profound truth underlying the simplicity of his answer. 'At the end of the day it's part of who we are.' It is part of belonging, part of what connects us, part of our identity.

Identity and belonging are central to the sacramentality of the rite of baptism. We are reminded in Luke's Gospel that the event of Jesus' baptism is a moment of revelation of his identity. Jesus is clearly, visibly and publicly identified as the anointed one – the Christ, the Messiah, the beloved Son of God.

The ritual immersions performed by John on the banks of the River Jordan were baptisms of repentance and conversion. As the Son of God, Jesus was in no need of either. In coming to John for baptism however, Jesus identified himself as being unified with all those John had baptised, and with all of humanity. Jesus is one with those he had come to save.

Similarly, our baptism identifies us as being one with God and one with God's people. Our identity is from God and 'of God'. Through the transformative waters of baptism, we are called by our name and identified as unique individuals. We are baptised into the life and love of the Creator, the Christ and the Spirit.

The presence of the triune God at the baptism of the Lord signifies the start of Jesus' public ministry, and simultaneously sets him on the path to Calvary. From above the waters of the Jordan, Jesus is affirmed by the Creator and strengthened by the Spirit. Our baptism therefore, identifies us as being one with the Trinity, and as such, calls us to mission. 'Part of who we are' then, is being a people of prophecy, a people of dialogue. In the words of American theologian Fr Stephen Bevans, mission is our 'divine invitation to join the dance'.[1]

The recent General Assembly of the Fifth Plenary Council of Australia reiterated the significance of this invitation in committing the Church in Australia to 'being centred on Christ, with a baptismal identity and on a path of missionary discipleship'.[2]

Similarly, themes of communion, participation and mission are echoed Pope Francis' call to the 2023 Synod in Rome. The preparatory documentation restates the significance of our baptismal call to mission:

> All of God's people share a common dignity and vocation through baptism. We are all called to be active participants in the life of the Church. We can never be centred on ourselves. Our mission is to witness to the love of God in the midst of the whole human family... especially with those who live on the spiritual, social, economic, political, geographical, and existential peripheries of our world.[3]

The deep humility of both Jesus and John, evident in Luke's Gospel, provides a blueprint for a culture of mission. Jesus, in identifying himself as being one with humanity, and John in proclaiming his unworthiness for the task he has been assigned. Like Mary, both have said 'yes' to God's invitation, aware that it will call more from them than they feel they have to give. Likewise, God's unconditional love that has been gifted to us, is strengthened in us through our baptism.

We are reminded in Genesis 12:2 of the beautiful Abrahamic notion that those who are blessed are then called to be a blessing. The gentle wisdom of these words sets our course. We are continually blessed by God through others and through the world around us. Sometimes we become so preoccupied with the busyness of life, we miss the simplicity and beauty of these blessings, and we also miss opportunities to respond to others with love and compassion.

Life's blessings are generally not epochal events – Damascus or Emmaus moments. They are an incremental dawning of the beauty and wonder of people and of creation; of the work of God in the world today. The 2021 Senior Australian of the Year, Dr Miriam Rose Ungunmerr Baumann stresses the importance of *dadirri* – that deep listening and silent awareness, of taking the time to listen, and of finding God in the smallest of the natural wonders around us.[4]

The lilies of the field are a blessing; the newborn baby is a blessing; the relative in the dementia ward is a blessing. These blessings are a whisper of grace in our lives. We need to be attuned to listening for them, and responding with love, so that we in turn can be a blessing for others. That is our baptismal call. That is our mission. That is 'part of who we are'.

Little Ivy is now an energetic and inquisitive toddler, fully engaged with the world and all it holds for her. The significance of her baptismal call is yet to be revealed to her. She is blessed, and she is an absolute blessing to all who come her way. Ivy belongs, she is connected, and she is loved. She is part of who we are.

## NOTES

1. Bevans S, *The mission has a church: an invitation to the dance*, Yarra Theological Union, Melbourne, 2009.
2. Costelloe T & Mackinlay S, *Fifth Plenary Council of Australia: Called by Christ – Sent Forth as Missionary Disciples*, Fifth Plenary Council of Australia, Decree 3, July 2022, accessed 21 August 2022.
3. Synod of Bishops, For a Synodal Church: Communion, Participation, and Mission, 'Vademecum for the Synod on Synodality, Secretary General of the Synod of Bishops', https://www.synod.va/en/news/the-vademecum-for-the-synod-on-synodality.html, 7 September 2021, accessed 21 August 2022.
4. Ungunmerr Baumann MR, 'Dadirri: Inner Deep Listening and Quiet Still Awareness', Emmaus Productions, 2022, https://www.miriamrosefoundation.org.au/dadirri, accessed 21 August 2022.

**TEMPUS C**
**8th SUNDAY**

# Getting Real and Getting On With It
### Luke 6:39–45

#### KATE ENGLEBRECHT

I want to begin with a story about a woman named Mary* I met when I was offering pastoral care to isolated palliative patients in far Western NSW. I had the privilege of getting to know a wonderfully alive, thoroughly authentic, very real woman who was dying with a particularly brutal sort of brain tumour. She'd lived an especially hard and challenging life, full of both joy and suffering.

Mary had grown up on a farm and had fed sheep through endless gruelling droughts. She was married to a man she loved dearly and lived in a modest home on the edge of a small rural town. Hers was a simple life and faith. She was frank, direct, and always honest. Lying on her bed connected to various intravenous lines, she would often talk to me about God, Jesus, and life in Christ.

She knew:
> that truth needs quiet before it can be spoken
> that it takes courage to trust lived experience
> that the fear of suffering can be worse that the reality of it
> that we don't always have to control what is happening
> that the person you are today is not the person you were yesterday
> that relationships are infinitely more complex than anyone could possibly imagine
> that nothing lasts forever
> that not a great deal actually matters in the end.

*not her real name

She knew that what lasts and lives is love.

Mary chose transformation above preservation and had the courage to speak about what was happening when despair might have been so much easier. There was no pretence about her, and she was often quite hard on herself as she looked back on her life. She didn't want to be dying but she wasn't fighting a 'battle' with malignant cells or trying to 'beat the odds' either. Mary wasn't expecting a miracle or lighting candles. She was always realistic and grounded in what was happening. In moments of quiet examination of her life, she was often quite critical but never judged herself too harshly. For Mary, life and death offered a chance to get real, to face what had to be faced.

Luke 6:39–45 deals with getting real and getting on with it. Luke invites us to be challenged by the experience of Jesus, to do what has to be done and live life in a new way.

What we hear from Scripture depends a great deal on what we are listening and looking for. I seek to know myself better through Luke's parable so that I might remove 'the log' from my own eye, to 'get real', so that my discipleship might become deep and authentic.

Believing that Scripture is as much about the art of listening and ruminating – of story-telling, literature, narrative, imagery, symbol, poetry, metaphor, and myth – I wonder what it might take at a spiritual level to get real. What it might mean to see the log in my own eye, and not be fixated on 'the speck' in my neighbour's; to know 'the good treasure of the heart'.

Jesus invites his disciples to learn, amongst other things, the meaning of suffering and the necessity to live true to his teachings. In the context of his parables, he encourages them to grow up in their faith, to know their own need for transformation and dare to live courageously and radically. In their ministry of leadership, the disciples were required to take responsibility and to recognise what was counterfeit and illusory in themselves, and in others. They faced the challenge of ending old ways of thinking and behaving. They were called to be honest and to live a radical life of self-knowledge, inner transformation and forgiveness, despite their own shortcomings and weaknesses. The disciples were teachers who could draw on wells of wisdom, only because they had plumbed those depths of spiritual compunction and walked through the darkness beneath. They needed to choose spiritual life over the ego's instinct for power and survival.

Luke 6:39–45 contributes to the message that saying the right thing is not enough, one must be the truth of the Good News. If the Gospel is about authenticity, integrity, and honesty, I wonder what it really takes to be a woman disciple and leader in the Church today. What do spiritual depth, maturity and authenticity look like for us today? How do we and so many other women who teach and serve others in the name of Christ, draw goodness from good treasure in our own hearts? Why is it so hard to step away from the false, illusory, egoistic self? Why does following Jesus often feel so much like a sort of dying? How are we to begin to trust the letting go of the false self to allow something less judgemental and more authentic to emerge? Crucially, how much has that false self been formed by the experiences of oppression and rejection by run-of-the-mill, everyday patriarchy?

The answers to these questions belong within the context of a real and genuine desire for self-knowledge. We need to trust in the guidance of Luke, Mary Magdelene and our other contemplative, prophetic women Saints in their experiences of prayer and union with the Divine. We must be prepared to take a good, long, hard look at our own lives every now and then and own what we see. We must remember that we can't lead anyone anywhere that we're not prepared to go ourselves.

My friend Mary was – with Luke and Mary Magdalene and other prophetic women – far from perfect. Like them though, she knew something of the 'log' in her own eye, she knew something of her own formation. She was real and authentic and, knowing how dark the road could be, she desired to follow Jesus all the way.

These are disciples to be trusted. They knew what it took to drop the false self and face the truth and the paradox of their own brokenness, their own powerlessness. They knew that the deepest part of themselves was Christ living within them. Prayerfully, they drew what was good from that inner Self, and from that silent place, drew those around them into the great Ground of Being, into the Divine Indwelling God, the compassionate Universal, cosmic living Heart of the whole World.

It might take the rest of our lives to know our blind spots better, to recognise the logs in our own eyes, to understand the forces that have formed us. It might take us years to begin to know ourselves more deeply, to truly meet the Christ who is utterly at home in all that 'woman experience'. It might take each of us even longer to find the responses that will begin to transform our lives, but the desire to begin the task again and again is as important as any goal.

So, what might Luke 6:39–45 ask of us today? We are prophets, preachers and priests, perhaps we just need to live more honestly and face the truth of our lives more courageously. To ask ourselves the right questions. To be people open to constant conversion, constant movement in the Spirit, liberated by the love of Christ.

Let us Pray:

> May we know ourselves more deeply and see our own blind spots more clearly.
>
> May we – with Mary the mother of God – give birth to Christ in our own lives and then, transformed by Love, let go and be brave enough to 'get on with it'.
>
> May we – like Mary Magdalene – trust in the truth of our vocation and be the agents of change and transformation we are commissioned to be by the Risen Christ, for the sake of the whole world.
>
> Amen.

**TEMPUS C**
**16th SUNDAY**

# Jesus Visits Martha and Mary
## Luke 10:38–42

GEMMA THOMSON

WITH REFLECTIONS FROM RILEY-JAYNE CARROLL & SAMARA SPADANUDA

I am privileged to work at Iona Presentation College, a Catholic School in the Presentation tradition, located between river and sea in Mosman Park, Western Australia, where I have the opportunity to plant seeds of faith with our inspiring young women. I have the pleasure of nurturing their spirituality during their high-school years; walking with them as they question, wonder and pray. As a young lay woman myself, I pray I can inspire these young women to treasure their faith journey and relationship with God at a time when it is often counter-cultural for young people.

Teaching Religious Education is a true calling, and two of my Year 12 Religion and Life students, Riley-Jayne, and Samara, joined me in preparing this reflection. When I posed the opportunity to the girls, like Mary they quickly said 'Yes!' Riley-Jayne and Samara have been committed to service and the faith life of the College, acting as important role models for their peers. Additionally, the thoughts by Ann Marie of the Busy Blessed Women blog[1] enriched our conversation and reflections.

> Now as they went on their way, he entered a certain village, where a woman named Martha welcomed him into her home. She had a sister named Mary, who sat at the Lord's feet and listened to what he was saying. But Martha was distracted by her many tasks; so she came to him and asked, 'Lord, do you not care that my sister has left me to do all the work by myself? Tell her then to help me.' But the Lord answered her, 'Martha, Martha, you are worried and distracted by many things; there

is need of only one thing. Mary has chosen the better part, which will not be taken away from her.' (Luke 10:38–42)

Martha and Mary were not only part of Jesus' friendship network, but also women in a culture where religious leaders did not openly engage in such friendships. Reflecting on the sacred text, there are three key life-lessons that can be learnt from this Gospel.

First, we learn that hospitality is a free gift; we are called to open our hearts and offer hospitality to others, no matter the circumstances.

The gospel states that Martha 'welcomed' Jesus 'into her home', which alludes to the fact that she owned the home. Some believe that Martha was the older sister and as a result, was used to being in charge. The eldest sibling is generally the one who creates precedents for the younger siblings, the reliable one who is the 'glue' of the family, and who naturally takes on the protector role.

We learn that Martha invited Jesus and the guests in; they were unannounced. We can fall into the trap of thinking 'Oh, the house isn't spotless' or 'I don't have suitable food to offer' and would prefer to know people are visiting in advance. Instead, unannounced visits, like that of Jesus in this story, are often a blessing. When Martha says to Jesus 'Lord, do you not care that my sister has left me to do all the work by myself? Tell her then to help me' (v.40), she expresses frustration that she was doing all the hostess work while her sister was listening to Jesus. We learn from today's gospel that acts of service and hospitality are a true mark of discipleship (demonstrated by Martha), but they must be grounded in Jesus' love (demonstrated by Mary).

Secondly, we must be alert to the twenty-first century 'comparison trap'. Whether we are a 'Martha' or a 'Mary', we all have inherent dignity, value and purpose in this world.

As young women today, our lives are a web of comparison, whether we like it or not. Social media platforms such as Facebook, Instagram and Tik Tok evoke emotional responses where young people measure their self-worth or success in comparison to others. To enter a tertiary educational institution, our academic achievement is compared to other students' to determine places. In navigating twenty-first century relationships and friendships, the status quo of what is expected between two people is often a point of comparison. It is too easy to become troubled or worried about other's behaviours and we can become self-righteous and judgmental.

Therefore the onus is on us to act with courage and consciously remove ourselves from this comparison trap. Through the personalities of Martha and Mary, we realise that each of us has our own personality and purpose, valuable and full of God-honouring promise. We are reminded that all of us have our own stories to craft, our own tapestries of life to weave; we might not all conclude our stories on the same page. The only thing that we all have in common is that our life stories have the same author: we don't know what the future holds, but we know who holds the future.

Thirdly, we are reminded that examining our priorities in life is vital. In our increasingly busy world, we need to make time to be present to Jesus.

Examining the interaction between the two sisters in this Gospel, Martha wanted Mary to behave in what was traditionally understood as a woman's role of that time and place. It was uncommon for women to listen to rabbis teach. Instead of helping her sister Martha with the domestic chores, Mary consciously chose to listen to Jesus. Her choice to do this was a definite sign to all of us.

We are called to consider: am I a Martha or a Mary in my relationship with Jesus? Earlier in this reflection, we mentioned the physical location of our school, Iona, as being between 'river and sea'. This poses an image of the relationship between Martha and Mary, with Jesus holding them in creative tension. The two sisters chose two very different actions and the way that Jesus reacted to their choices is a life lesson for us all. Do I have my priorities in order? Like Martha, am I worried or anxious about many things? Or, like Mary, am I focused on listening to Jesus and spending time in his presence? In some reflections, Martha has been compared to the Apostle Peter: practical, impulsive, and short-tempered to the point of rebuking the Lord himself. Mary is described as more like the Apostle John: reflective, loving and calm. Even so, Martha is a remarkable woman and deserves considerable credit.

Some of us tend to be more like Mary in our Christian journeys and some like Martha. It is likely we have qualities of both within us as part of our unique ways of being. The following verse in the Gospel is a life lesson about priorities: 'Martha, Martha, you are worried and distracted by many things; there is need of only one thing. Mary has chosen the better part, which will not be taken away from her' (v.41–42).

Being a disciple of Jesus, sitting at his feet to listen is not lazy; in fact, it is what we are called to do in whatever shape or form that occurs for us in our lives. 'Sitting at the feet of Jesus' is about spending time to learn about Jesus so that we can be more like him in our daily interactions with others. We are called to be do-ers of The Word and not hearers only. Our foundress, Venerable Nano Nagle's family motto was 'Deeds, not words': this integrates perfectly with the notion of committing ourselves to prioritising time for Jesus. Like Jesus, Nano knew the importance of carrying out lantern work by day, but spending time in contemplative prayer with God of an evening. Listening deeply to the Word of God and the indwelling Spirit is just as important as being people of action.

Mary prioritised listening to Jesus over chores. Jesus ignored the traditional role of women at that time and acknowledged Mary's desire to listen and learn. He also made it clear that service was important in his ministry, honouring Martha too. Above all, we learn that being a disciple of Jesus comes first. We are reminded that good works flow from a Christ-centred life; they do not in themselves produce a Christ-centred life. When we give Jesus the attention he deserves in our lives, we can empower others, using our God-given gifts and talents. Like Mary, we are called to find fellowship with our God. Through the Word of God, fellowship, discipleship, prayer and worship, our spirit is enriched and God will provide – 'all will be well, and all manner of things will be well'[2].

May your God who knows and loves you, bless you abundantly and may you be inspired by the gifts of both Martha and Mary, in their interaction with Jesus in this gospel reflection.

## NOTES

1. Busy Blessed Women, *The Story of Mary and Martha*, https://busyblessedwomen.com/the-story-of-mary-and-martha/, accessed 5 December 2022.
2. Julian, Anchoress at Norwich, *Revelations of Divine Love*, Gutenberg Project, accessed 8 December 2022.

## REFERENCES

Busy Blessed Women, https://busyblessedwomen.com
Julian, Anchoress at Norwich, *Revelations of Divine Love*, Gutenberg Project

**TEMPUS C**
**17th SUNDAY**

# What God Offers in Answer to Prayer
### Luke 11:1–13

MOIRA BYRNE

This passage contains a few avenues to explore, but I will focus on the beginning and the end. At the start, Jesus teaches prayer, and we can grasp another purpose. The end of the reading prompts us to consider how God responds to prayer requests. This is, for me, the most interesting and challenging part of the scripture, because it provokes me to consider unanswered prayers.

Across Christian churches, the Lord's Prayer is often said verbatim. My parish has a wonderful custom of holding one another's hands as we pray. We speak the words together and pray as one community and it's beautiful.

Yet I can't help but wonder if shared prayer is extra to Jesus' intended purpose. To me, the order of the prayer seems more like a guide on how to start and maintain a meaningful relationship.

'Father, hallowed be your name': we name people and place them in our lives; we compliment them, and express our gratitude for them.

'Your kingdom come': we hope they achieve their purpose and wish them well in fulfilling their mission and in flourishing as people.

'Give us each day our daily bread': we communicate clearly our own needs and wants.

'And forgive us our sins for we ourselves forgive everyone indebted to us': we open avenues for communication and ask forgiveness when we've made an error, and we also forgive them. We try to be generous as we maintain the relationship.

'And do not bring us to the time of trial': we seek truth and keep each other safe from the things that will harm us as we pursue our wholeness. We try to understand each other and make the best we can of difficult circumstances.

> And we can add the traditional ending to the Our Father prayer:
> For the kingdom, the power and the glory are yours, now
> and forever: we wish the best for them, always.

So, as Jesus teaches us to pray, he shows how to start, grow and maintain a relationship with our creator.

Later, in Luke 11:9, Jesus tells us: 'Ask, and it will be given you; search, and you will find; knock, and the door will be opened for you.' For me this is a much more difficult part of the gospel. I've always been deeply uncomfortable with the kind of 'shopping list' prayer that 'names and claims' favours from God – 'If you didn't receive enough, it's because you didn't believe enough'. There is something selfish and transactional about that prayer. It is demanding and entitled.

I don't think God operates that way and it paints a problematic portrait of God. Rather, God is love, as it says in 1 John.[1] God is truth, as it says in John 14.[2] And God is transcendent, as it says in Acts[3], and the Hebrew Scriptures.[4]

For me, prayer is a relationship that allows us to love deeply and be changed and refined by deep love.

And as this project, Australian Women Preach, is about Scripture through the lens of women's experience, I can share how my understanding of God and prayer changed when I first became a mother.

My husband and I were excited to learn we were having a baby. Like all new parents of faith, we prayed for my smooth pregnancy and a healthy bub. And like most people who pray this, it's not just for a baby without disease. By default, it's a prayer for a baby without disability.

That was not to be. I had a near miscarriage, but we were relieved that the rest of the pregnancy went okay. Though the labour and birth were difficult, I delivered our beautiful baby girl – only she was not bouncing. At an early stage she failed to thrive, but it was only in the months and year afterwards that we came to understand our daughter was disabled.

This changed our faith profoundly. How could we make sense of this? I'd never thought God was a puppeteer making things happen – we have free will. And I'd never wondered why tragedies happened to some people. Yet when this happened in our life I kept asking: 'Why my daughter, why me, and why us? Did we do something wrong? What?'

We worked through this, amid both dreadful insensitivity and wise and loving support, and came to understand that God was with us, in relationship with us on our journey of life. Loving us, loving through each other, and encouraging us to love and not be afraid. As a friend of mine said: you love your child, however they arrive. You love a baby with an illness, or a disability – because they are yours. And it's true.

I'm thankful that this was a crisis of faith my husband and I endured together. His character, our vulnerability and openness with each other, and our shared dreams for ourselves and one another meant this became an opportunity to grow even closer.

In more recent years I've realised that such trials are not something I would change, even if I could. I cannot deny that having a child who does not communicate in any conventional ways, who uses a wheelchair and requires support in every aspect of her life has posed challenges. But I might not have been brave enough to adopt some of the choices we made if things had been different. And I might not be as compassionate towards others enduring heartache. We might not have moved interstate, or met the people we did, or had personal opportunities to pursue our goals and support each other to do so. We might not have involved ourselves in advocacy.

And would our family dynamic be different? Our subsequent children are accepting and loving, and they see unique positive gifts that everyone can bring. The experience and wisdom developed through questioning and hardships might have given us those personal qualities that led to meaning and accomplishment over our lives.

So maybe the insight is that what God offers in answer to prayer is beyond my imagination. Of course, that includes my own mindset: 'all things work together for good for those who love God, who are called according to his purpose'.[5]

God's purpose is love, and truth, and hope, and clarity, and healing, and wholeness, and salvation and freedom from sin and darkness.

It's particular to Luke's gospel that Jesus talks about giving the Spirit rather than giving gifts after prayer.[6] We may request something in particular, but better yet, we receive the Spirit who transforms everything into a gift.

Hard experiences in our lives can be transformed if we can respond with love, not fear. We can use them to find ways to bring others love, truth, hope, clarity, healing, wholeness, salvation and freedom.

How? By maintaining relationships: both with our creator and our community. We can be grateful, even for difficulties, because things work together for good if we want them to, with time and effort.

The scripture says God would not answer a prayer request with something unhelpful. Yet we can appreciate that God, through our own wishes and wants and openness to growth, can offer us much more.

This resonates with another gospel story of God the Father, the prodigal son.[8] A 'just' father might begrudgingly allow his wayward son to return as a servant, but instead he dresses him in finery and lays on a welcome home banquet.[9]

So ... what if I ask for bread, but am offered a feast? What if our unanswered prayers are actually an invitation to let go of a shopping list and focus on a relationship with God? If we seek God's purpose, God will give us more than we can dream of.

## NOTES

1. 'God is love, and those who abide in love abide in God, and God abides in them', 1 John 4:16.
2. 'I am the way, the truth and the life', John 14:6.
3. 'The God who made the world and everything in it ... does not live in shrines made by human hands', Acts 17:24.
4. 'But who is able to build him a house, since heaven, even highest heaven, cannot contain him?' 2 Chronicles 2:6. 'For my thoughts are not your thoughts, nor are your ways my ways, says the Lord. For as the heavens are higher than the earth, so are my ways higher than your ways and my thoughts than your thoughts.' Isaiah 55:8–9.
5. Romans 8:28
6. If we 'know how to give good gifts' to our children, 'how much more will the heavenly Father give the Holy Spirit to those who ask', Luke 11:13.
7. Luke 15:11–32
8. Luke 11:11
9. Luke 15:22–24

TEMPUS C
19th SUNDAY

# Lighting Our Lamps and Standing with Those Who Have No Agency
### Luke 12:32–48

#### CHRISTINE REDWOOD

When I read Luke 12:32–48, I feel uncomfortable. I know it's Jesus telling these stories, but let's be clear, these are stories about slaves. A lot of translations soften that word and use 'servant' instead. As Luke 12:35–36 states:

> Be dressed for action and have your lamps lit; be like those who are waiting for their master to return from the wedding banquet, so that they may open the door for him as soon as he comes and knocks.

Servants or slaves, waiting. Slaves were common in the ancient world and had little agency. They were someone's property, which means they were disposable. Exploited. Almost a commodity, benefiting the one who owned them. For those who are not enslaved, their eyes would skim past them, barely notice that they were there, and barely consider them unless they were not doing the work they should be doing. It was not shocking to see blows fall on slaves' bodies. Flogging, sexual abuse, torture – it was all possible.

Yet Jesus calls those who want to be his disciples to identify with the slave. Ready for service, lamps burning as you wait for the master to return (v.35). This is a strange position that we might not be used to occupying. Do you know what it's like not to have power? Eyes skimming past and over you as if you weren't there? Blows falling on your body? Some of us do.

Women have often found themselves with little agency. For a long time, women were considered a man's property. Things have changed, but those gendered expectations go deep, don't they? Many women know what it is to do most of the domestic work, keeping the lamps burning. Attentive to others and meeting their needs. Women also, unfortunately, know about violence. Domestic violence is still alarmingly high, along with sexual violence. It is not unusual to see blows fall on women's bodies.

Of course, this is what makes these parables so uncomfortable. When you identify with the slave, it gets you thinking about the history of slavery with which we are still reckoning. We categorise those who are disposable, ripe for exploitation, a commodity to do the work beneath us – and those who deserve dignity, respect, authority and power. There are still workers exploited today. People trafficked. Women forced into marriage. Children labouring instead of in school. People stuck in debt bondage they can never escape. Toiling away to make a lot of the commodities we enjoy. Our clothes, coffee, and technology pass through their hands. Our eyes skim over them, ignoring the blows to their bodies.

Jesus is teaching the crowds. He is teaching who God is and what it means to be a disciple. As he comes to the end of this great teaching, he gives these two parables that put the slave front and centre. He says, 'Be dressed, slaves, ready for service, keep the lamps burning. I have good news for you. The master is coming. He is not what you are expecting. When he comes, he is going to dress like a slave. He is going to identify with the slave and serve the slaves. He will invite the slaves to the table, where they can relax and eat. The roles will be reversed. Be ready'.

Peter, one of Jesus' disciples, listening to this parable, is confused. Peter is not a slave. So, he asks: 'Is this for the crowd? For the slaves in the crowd? For me personally?' Jesus answers by telling a second story about a slave with a little more power than the other slaves. This slave is like a manager, in charge of the other slaves while the master is away. He's meant to look out for them. Jesus warns that if the manager thinks the master is taking a long time to return and begins beating the other slaves, raining blows onto their vulnerable bodies, taking their food and drink, then when the master returns, that manager will be punished. Cut into pieces. If the manager, for some reason, didn't realise what the master would wish, the punishment will be less severe. All this talk of beating wouldn't have made Peter flinch. This is what he'd expect. This is what makes me want to turn away from this parable. Why is Jesus talking about beatings and people being cut off? Maybe he needs to get Peter's attention. Jesus is calling on Peter to identify with this slave. Perhaps Peter does flinch after all! This second parable is a warning for those who have agency and power and knowledge about God and God's ways – to think carefully about how you will use such power.

By confronting and bringing back the word 'slave' into these parables and identifying with the slaves I have started to see Jesus doing what he so often does. Taking something familiar and known in his world, like slavery, and subverting it. 'Be dressed for action and have your lamps lit; be like those who are waiting for their master to return from the wedding banquet…If he comes during the middle of the night, or near dawn, and finds them so, blessed are those slaves.'

The first parable Jesus tells is, in many ways, about himself: what it means for him to be the Son of Man, and it is startling. Jesus is not what people expect. Jesus' eyes do not skim past us. Jesus sees those at the bottom of the social order. He sees those who are exploited and mistreated. He wants to give them, gives us, a seat at his table. We are welcome. Jesus is also preparing his disciples for his death. He is saying: don't despair for that won't be the end. There will be an absence, but when I return, all the old social divisions will fall apart. We will eat together. Okay, you might think, something to look forward to in the future, but what about now?

That's where the second parable comes in. It is speaking about living in the world now. Jesus suggests we will be held to account for how we live. If we know that in Jesus' eyes, every person is welcomed to his table, if we know that people are not disposable or objects to be used, if we know that God comes to serve us, shouldn't that change how we live now? Especially for those of us with power and agency and knowledge of who Jesus is. We have a responsibility to care for those who are vulnerable. Having identified ourselves as slaves might move us even further. So, we say – this whole system of master and slave is not right. Nobody should be exploited. No more blows raining down on another person's body. This is what a disciple of Jesus does. We light our lamps and stand with those who have no agency as we wait. We declare: Jesus is coming.

## REFERENCES

Anti-Slavery Australia, https://antislavery.org.au/modern-slavery/, date accessed 5 December, 2022.

Baird J, 'The Church Stripped Bare: High Rate of Domestic Abuse among Anglicans Exposed', *Sydney Morning Herald*, June 12, 2021.

Dowling E, 'Slave Parables in the Gospel of Luke: Gospel "Texts of Terror"?' *Australian Biblical Review 56*, 2008, pp 61–68.

Gafney, WC, *Womanist Midrash: A Reintroduction to the Women of the Torah and the Throne*, Louiseville, John Knox Press, 2017.

**TEMPUS C**
**20th SUNDAY**

# 'I come to bring division'
## Luke 12:49–53

### MICHELLE EASTWOOD

The reading for the 20th Sunday of Ordinary time Year C is found in Luke 12:49–53. Just four short verses, and yet I must admit that there is much about this reading that I don't understand. The statement that Jesus has come to cast fire on the earth is clearly metaphorical and brings to mind images of the refiners fire (Malachi 3:3; Proverbs 17:3; Hebrews 12:29) – a fire that is incredibly hot, and that burns away impurities. However, it is unclear to me how this statement relates to the teachings that come before or after it.

It is followed by another interesting claim: 'I have a baptism with which to be baptised and what stress I am under until it is completed!' (Luke 12:50). I am not a New Testament scholar, and I can't read this text in Greek. I do not claim to know what to do with this statement. For what it's worth, I think that the church would be much healthier if we were more willing to admit we don't always understand the meaning of these ancient Scriptures.

Therefore, it is the second section of the reading that I am going to reflect on. In verses 51–53 it says:

> [51] Do you think that I have come to bring peace to the earth? No, I tell you, but rather division! [52] 'From now on five in one household will be divided, three against two and two against three; [53] they will be divided:
> father against son
> and son against father,
> mother against daughter
> and daughter against mother,

> mother-in-law against her daughter-in-law
> and daughter-in-law against mother-in-law.'

Luke presents this statement as part of a series of teachings that Jesus gives on his way to Jerusalem. At the start of the chapter Jesus is addressing a crowd, although only slightly before these verses, Peter asks if Jesus is talking to the crowd or to the disciples (Luke 12:41). Without other clarification, it remains unclear the intended audience for this particular part of the message.

The parallel teaching in Matthew's re-telling is during the sending out of the disciples (Matthew 10:34–36). This makes much more sense because the message that the disciples are being instructed to bring, may very well be divisive. This is true in a contemporary context, too.

Within the Lutheran Church of Australia, the issue of women's ordination has been debated for many years. There are many who believe that this issue will split the church.

The acceptance of two understandings of marriage within the Uniting Church of Australia – that is, marriage is between two people, and that marriage is between a woman and a man – is also seen as a threat to unity.

These are just two contemporary Australian examples that demonstrate division within the church. Further, the range of churches and denominations that exist throughout history and in the world today, within what the Nicene Creed calls the 'one Catholic and apostolic church' demonstrates that division has always been part of our story. Many of these diverse churches claim that they have the truth, and that only they know what God really means and wants, as opposed to the church down the road who does things a little differently.

Once we are sure we know what God wants, it is easy to denounce anyone who thinks differently and to find a biblical reference to back our perspective up.

However, what I find really interesting in this passage is the examples used about who will be in conflict: fathers and sons, mothers and daughters, mothers-in-law and daughters-in-law. This is a very gendered list. And it goes from those who have most cultural and social authority, to those who have least.

If I were to try to explain it, I would suggest that fathers and sons potentially have conflict over who has the greater authority. In my work on ageing, the giving over of authority from one generation to another is potentially an ongoing source of conflict. As the son grows and has a family of his own, he may want more authority in the family than the father is willing to give – this is especially true if everyone is living in the same house. The father may not recognise his declining capacity and/or authority and the son may be impatient to be the boss.

Mothers are perhaps less likely to have conflict with their sons. Rather, the conflict may be with her daughters as she prepares them to live in another family's house. This brings to mind the quarrel between Daphne and Violet Bridgerton – mother and daughter – in the popular Bridgerton book series. Daphne accuses Violet of not preparing her adequately for marriage – particularly in terms of what to expect on her wedding night. I can relate to Violet wanting to protect Daphne (and her other daughters). Violet struggles with her own discomfort when talking about the difficult subject of marital intimacy. There is every chance she wasn't well prepared and therefore she perpetuates taboos around talking about sex, particularly the potential pleasures of sexuality and sexual expression.

In raising my own children, I was very aware that I held much more anxiety for my daughter than for my sons. This was because I knew the pressures that are placed on young women in our patriarchal world – even while acknowledging that these limits are not fair nor reasonable.

The tension between a mother-in-law and her daughter-in-law is often the basis of horror stories and misogynistic jokes. These women are often seen as vying for the attention of the son/husband and fighting over the 'correct' way of running a household.

I think this mimics the wider move which frequently pits women against each other in competition for men's approval. In this framework, one woman is seen as the winner, which means the other is a loser. I suggest that this competition means that everyone ends up losing.

In this text, Luke may be quoting Micah 7:5–6. In Micah, these oppositions are placed within an oracle of judgement. It reads:

> Put no trust in a friend;
> have no confidence in a loved one;
> guard the doors of your mouth from her who lies in your embrace,
> ⁶for the son treats the father with contempt,
> the daughter rises up against her mother,
> the daughter-in-law against her mother-in-law;
> your enemies are members of your own household.

In this passage, the younger partner is presented as fighting against the elder. This brings to mind perennial cross-generational complaints about the disrespectful, lazy, younger generations. Currently, it is the Millennials judged thus, although growing up I remember these criticisms targeted at Generation X.

In the Micah reading, godlessness is to blame for the division within families, not the message of God. So, is division because of God's message or because people have turned away from God? Or is division just part of the human experience?

If we return to the Garden of Eden, the very first consequence of eating the fruit is that Eve and Adam hide themselves from each other and from God. Before eating, they are naked and unashamed. They have no need to cover up or place a barrier between themselves. After eating the fruit, the vines hide their perceived flaws and vulnerabilities. Perhaps this applies to the Lukan passage as well.

Perhaps the division is not about God's message, but about the way the message makes us feel. It may make us feel self-righteous, affirmed, convinced that we know what God wants. Alternatively, it might make us feel unworthy, ashamed, not good enough, and desiring to hide away. Of course, it could be a mixture of these and other feelings.

And the feelings probably have as much to do with messages we have received about God, about the church and about Christianity as they do about God's actual message – assuming that as humans we even have the capacity to understand God's message completely and without distortion.

Perhaps this is why the fire is needed. The refining fire burns away the dross that humans have added to the message, then we are left with the core ingredient – love. Love which transcends all division and includes and affirms all. And perhaps Baptism is a public acknowledgement that all should be welcome and safe in this community. Perhaps one day, our churches, our communities and our world will also be able to move beyond the divisions and see the value inherent in every single person.

## REFERENCE

Quinn, J, *The Duke & I*, Avon, New York, USA, 2020.

**TEMPUS C**
**28th SUNDAY**

# Gratitude
## Luke 17:11–19

### Angela McCarthy

The readings for the 28th Sunday in Ordinary Time Year C offer us two stories about cures from the dreaded disease, leprosy. In 2 Kings 5:14–17, Naaman, a powerful Aramean warrior, is cured through the mediation of Elisha. Written about 800 years later, Luke 17:11–19 contains the action of Jesus curing ten lepers. Both miracles take place, not in the land of God's chosen people, but in Samaria. The Samaritans were shunned by the Jews for their opposing beliefs, especially that God's temple was in Samaria, not in Jerusalem. The significant common element in these two healings from leprosy stories is the gratitude depicted in both. The psalm neatly ties these two stories together by proclaiming that the 'Lord has revealed to the nations his saving power' (Psalm 98:2).[1] Simeon, when he held the newborn Jesus in the Temple, declared that he would be a 'light for revelation to the Gentiles and for glory to your people Israel' (Luke 2:32).

The prophet Elisha cures the powerful warrior Naaman who then declares that the God of Israel is indeed the only real God. He takes earth from Israel back to his home so that he can worship the God of that land. Gods were still understood to be anchored to a particular place. Naaman is a powerful man, offering rich gifts and proud enough to get upset with Elisha when he asked him to do a simple thing, wash himself in the Jordan. But his life is changed by the experience, and he is grateful.

When we turn to Luke's account of this particular healing miracle, there are also some other things to discover. This miracle is not in any of the other gospels and so we know that it is part of Luke's particular theological narrative about Jesus. Jesus has been teaching his disciples while on the journey to Jerusalem. He has been teaching them about faith, and about being grateful that you can do the work that God has given you and not expect thanks. He uses the image of the slave in the household; they do what is required without expecting thanks.

Both issues surface in the story of the ten lepers. The one leper who returns, a Samaritan, praises God and prostrates himself at Jesus' feet. Jesus tells him that his faith has saved him, a perfect illustration from his previous teaching. Faith is a key element in being part of salvation. Salvation means being aware of our God who has set us free and a response to salvation is giving praise and thanks to God. Naaman gave praise and thanks and wished to continue, so he took two mule loads of earth from Israel back to his home country. Salvation in Luke is also about being set free from the burdens and restrictions of this world, not just in the world to come. Being set free from the addictions and distractions of this world which enables us to live in the kingdom of God.

The gratitude of the healed leper presents a different idea and one that urges us to dig deeper into this story. Jesus has taught the disciples not to expect gratitude and yet here he is asking for it: 'Were not ten made clean? But the other nine, where are they? Was none of them found to return and give praise to God except this foreigner' (v.17–18). Does God require our thanks in order to continue to do good things for us? Unlike Mark and Matthew, Luke lessens the emotional aspects of Jesus' character and yet here we have a sense of disappointment. Why has only a foreigner come back? Where are the others? Gratitude does matter.

Where does gratitude fit in the kingdom of God? A major theme in Luke is about the coming of the kingdom of God. It is not a geographical space, a future heavenly space, or a political space, but a place where God is evident in the behaviour of the people who inhabit the space, who form the community. People who are grateful, who know that they are saved, who know that God has set them free.

When children are small, we teach them gratitude. One of the first words we teach them is 'Ta!' Learning to say thank you in an appropriate way is part of our culture, part of our etiquette. We do not do it because we want to be thanked endless times during the day as we care for little ones, we do it because we know that it is important in human behaviour and in the kingdom of God.

Gratitude is also a theological theme. It teaches us something about God. The God part of us wants to spread good will and a sense of being loved and we know that a good way to do that is to be grateful. Part of being in the kingdom of God is being able to say thank you. It leads us to an openness to God's grace. Mary E. Moore talks about God's grace as being the 'throbbing heartbeat of God in the world'.[2] We must have faith to hear the heartbeat and we have to choose to be thankful. By choosing thankfulness we can defeat bitterness.

One of the things that saddens me today is the number of places that have to put up signs to encourage respect within that environment. When you ring Centrelink you are reminded that respect is necessary, and abuse will not be tolerated. There is a sign at the GP's office, there are signs in libraries and supermarkets. What has happened in our society that we need to ask for such respect? The absence of thankfulness. A contemporary idea of the importance of the individual cancels out social responsibility. If we want something we have every right to demand it with whatever demeanour we choose. An absence of grace.

When difficult episodes of our life occur, we must choose how we will respond to them. Recently I experienced cancer and the surgery and following treatment reduced me to a very vulnerable and frail human being. Through careful spiritual preparation and excellent medical care, I survived well and was cared for with unbounded love and tenderness by family and friends. My response at every turn was thankfulness. Throughout the experience I had the undoubted knowledge of God's presence during the worst times and the best. I was conscious of my salvation through the grace of God, that wonderful heartbeat of God in the world.

One of the things to be grateful for are the small, precious moments. When my husband suffered a very serious traffic accident, after weeks of recuperation in bed he was able to get out in the spring sunshine and enjoy a cup of coffee with me, pain-free. The experience was graced, we felt God's presence in the love that binds us and in the joy of being able to appreciate creation on a beautiful sunny morning. God's heartbeat was evident, and we were grateful.

In caring for the aged, it is critical that we choose thankfulness. It is critical that those being cared for choose to be thankful and those that care for them choose to do the same. While a carer might not demand thankfulness, as Jesus taught, it makes a difference when it is part of the social exchange. It lifts both the giver and the receiver; it is a moment of grace. It is difficult when a person suffering dementia can no longer be thankful, but being thankful for the person they once were can make all the difference. One of the effects is to bring about the kingdom of God in the world, to make our space one of grace where we can feel the heartbeat of God.

### NOTE

1. *Lectionary for Mass* © *1969*, Translation for the psalm responses by ICEL St Pauls Publications, St Pauls Publications, NSW, 2012, p 97.
2. Moore ME, 'Parenting Elders: Finitude, Gratitude, and Grace' in *Parenting as Spiritual Practice and Source for Theology: Mothering Matters*, Springer International Publishing AG, New York, 2018.

*Celebration*

CELEBRATION
CHRISTMAS

# CHRISTMAS
## John 1:1–18

ALISON OVEREEM

Weaving the word that is
sits within the First Peoples
of Australian Culture, Community and Family.

With intense pleasure,
I navigate this weaving of the threads of the flesh and the word,
as sister to sister – weaving the laritja (thread)
that sits in the ever-present basket from John 1:1–18.

We seek to lean into the hope
that is woven in these chapters, these stories, these callings.

I am a proud descendant of warrior woman, Fanny Cochrane Smith:
a woman strong in Faith, strong in Spirituality and Aboriginality.

Our Ancestors' voices are the word that calls us.
Weaving as a basket of oneness,
weaving together not one narrative at the cost of another.
All interwoven, all interconnected to her faith
in a Culture that was and continues to be
one basket of Creation, of birth.
Because of her, I can.
Because of her, we do.
Because of her, we see.
Because in the spring, everything is dancing.

Everything is dancing, in the birth of spring.

The flesh of the word
weaving through First People's spirituality.

We need to seek to speak the word
through the woven connections, the *laritja*.

In the creation of the basket,
and in our shared dwelling together,
as I live and work
from the traditional homelands of the Muwinina people,
I would like to pay respects to my elders past and present,
and acknowledge the Tasmanian Aboriginal Community
as the current and continuing custodians and keepers of the word.

The word of the stories of this island,
the word embedded on *Lutruwita* (Tasmania).
A basket of Culture.

On this day, from these lands, from these ancient lands,
the wisdom that sits on and calls
from *milaythina ningee* (Mother Earth),
calls us to see the word through the flesh
that weaves like a river amongst First Peoples.

A voice *rrala* (strong) being as one,
the inner basket of shared weavings
of the layers that rejoice within John 1:1–18,
weave through a lens of my ancestors,
my faith, my spirituality, and my calling.

I share the hope that in this sharing of the word,
the word becomes one woven thread of one basket:
the word, the message, inherent indeed in the flesh.
In John 1:1–18, again we are reminded
of the one presence of the Creator,

the interconnectedness, the oneness with Jesus,
forever present, forever connected.

As one in the word, in the flesh,
and indeed in the justice basket,
born of hope, justice, and equality –
embedded as one in vulnerability,
sitting as one in the whole of creation.
Not just the seen, but the felt and the word,
always abundant within and around us.

Let us reflect on that thread
for it is inherent in the thread of the word,
it sits in the abundance of all creation
of all new life, and the life and birth of our Saviour.

The interwoven threads of all creation
lie at the very *takila* (heart) of these verses
since the Creation of First Peoples,
their storylines, song-lines, customs and traditions,
their forever connections with place and time,
with country and indeed, with each other.

Walking the lands, living with the land –
being one with the lands and being one with each other.

Born of the Creator, forever present, forever there,
and the key to open the layers of the scriptures,
sit within the First People's wisdom.
The key to the layers of messages within John 1:1–18
indeed sit within First Peoples.

We honour the Creator,
and know the Creator was moving amongst us, beside us, through us,
well before the invasion of these lands they now call Australia.

The Creator gifted the lands, the trees, the waterways,
and the layers of interconnectedness on and above Mother Earth,
to First Peoples as caretakers.
The Creator gifted this privilege and responsibility to us,
as First Peoples, in oneness.

Just as our Creator and Jesus were oneness.
A oneness calling to the layers that sit on and with country,
and indeed reflect and sit on and within
the verses of John 1:1–18.
John feels and knows the *laritja* of the word,
he knows the layers are one,
as one in the creation and one in the calling.

All of us are called to oneness.
We as First Peoples,
we as *luna rrala* (strong women)
are the voices in the Christian community
that are called by the Creator
to walk the path planned.
First to be the flesh amongst the mob,
to be the whole in the story of Creation,
to be one through the word,
as the justice carriers of that word we seek.
In this, we speak to relationship –
relationship in the oneness of the Creator and Jesus.

A oneness in the Creator's relationship
with and through each other,
to work amongst, to be vulnerable,
to be willing to sacrifice but to rejoice –
rejoice in the shared basket of the birth of all Creation.
In the knowing, in the word, in the healing,
and in the flesh of First Peoples.

Praise be to the Creator
and thanks be to the wisdom and the knowledge
of the First Peoples of Australia.
   Amen

   Let us pray
for the woven word from the flesh
that is the First Peoples of the Lands now called Australia.

**CELEBRATION**
**PALM SUNDAY**

# Knowing, Being, Doing and Valuing
## John 12:1, 12–13 • Luke 22:14

### RACHEL MCLEAN, JENNIFER KING, TAMILYN AH KEE & ASHLEIGH UNG

### How to read this reflection

This reflection is written using Relationally Responsive Pedagogies that have been used to teach First Nations children for millennia. These Pedagogies are informed by First Nations ways of Knowing, Being, Doing and Valuing.[1] In order for you, the reader, to get the most out of this reflection, we invite you to pause, to be still and listen to the sound of your breath sustaining you.

As you become still, consider the country beneath your feet; the lands and waterways on which you live. The skies which you live under and travel through; the seas which wash on your shores or perhaps you float upon. If you are reading in Australia, these lands which you have just recalled, are those of the First Nations peoples. Take a moment now to honour, in your own way, the people who have called this place – and the place you are reading from – home for millennia.

This reflection has been written on Gimuy Walubara Yidinji and Yirrganydji country; the region now known as Cairns. The collaborators of this reflection stand in solidarity with the Uluru Statement from the Heart and affirm that these lands, seas, skies and waterways, were, are and always will be those of the First Nations peoples.

When we are still, we have the opportunity to listen deeply to who and how we are. As collaborators, this is what we did each time we sat together. In these moments of stillness, we were able to listen deeply to the presence of the Spirit, the ancient wisdom of the land and the inner murmurings of our hearts. Through this deep listening we arrived at these words.

Tamilyn's grandparents taught her how to be: how to sit and listen to each other, and to country. Each Sunday morning, Tamilyn would urge her Mum and siblings to join her at their grandparents' home so the family could go to church together. Going to church was one way of being with each other. The being that Tamilyn speaks of is more than a physical proximity – it is a way of inhabiting life. A way that is spiritual, emotional, physical and known. When you listen deeply, when you are truly present to the other, then you are being with them.

When we sat and listened to the readings for Palm Sunday during our first collaboration, we all felt a little overwhelmed. You could even say that the readings were difficult to sit and *be* with.

As we pondered how we could process the density of the Palm Sunday readings, we stilled our whirling minds by considering the country on which Jesus found himself during Holy Week. We imagined the roads that Jesus walked as he made his way to Jerusalem. We imagined what these roads were framed by: the fertile plains that sustained; the arid undulations of desert; and the mountains that caught the rain. With this connection to country, or a land link (as described in Relationally Responsive Pedagogies), we found it easier to make meaning of the texts.

In fact, it was the Antiphon, which is read at the beginning of a Catholic Eucharistic Mass on Palm Sunday, that piqued our interest. The Antiphon is unique as it combines excerpts from John's Gospel with verses from Psalm 23. This felt good to us. We saw it as a non-linear way of telling story. We thought the authors of the Mass were being creative and courageous in how they were inviting participants in the liturgy into the story.

As we were reflecting on this Antiphon, we couldn't help but recall how stories have been lost for many First Nations communities as a result of the Stolen Generations. The practices of politicians and people in power from the not-too-distant past have meant that processes for passing on culture in Australia have been broken. This has meant that some of Jen, Tamilyn and Ashleigh's elders have had to go looking for narrative in other places. Elders from other nations shared site markers and land links which now help tell the story of place, space and family. Sometimes the stories have been lost completely; the young unable to hear and retell the ancient stories, unable to learn and pass on lore.

The Entrance Antiphon says that 'the children ran to meet him'[2] and cried out with a loud voice, reciting words from the psalms. This struck us: the gift of the psalms being sung through the ages, the freedom of the children in the crowds. It brought us back to the now. It caused us to pause and reflect on these questions; perhaps you, too, might like to pause and consider them a while (they are at the end of this reflection).

❋ ❋ ❋

After entering Palm Sunday through the Antiphon, we felt a little more able to enter The Passion narrative, which in 2022 (Year C) was from the Gospel according to Luke. The Passion begins at the table (Luke 22:14); it is the table and the sharing of a feast that connected Ashleigh's family to the text. The beginning of the Passion reminded Ashleigh of Easters with her Grandma; a holy woman who found strength and solace in the church as well as in the ancient spirituality of the Wakaid Badulgal people. Just like those who prepared the food for the Last Supper, Ashleigh's Grandma always makes sure there is plenty of food; not just for their family, but whoever comes to the feast.

The radical sense of hospitality, like that shown by Ashleigh's Grandma, is a central theme of how the Gospel according to Luke is recounted. Brendan Byrne describes this gift of hospitality present in the Last Supper as follows:

> Believers of subsequent generations who participate in [the Eucharist] will recognise, when they see the broken bread and poured out wine that they are the beneficiaries of blessings stated here. They will experience the hospitality of God in full knowledge of its cost, cost not only to Jesus who gave himself up for them, but also cost to the Father who sent [Jesus into the world].[3]

The radical nature of this hospitality is not only in that which is laid on the table, but that which is laid at our feet. Ashleigh shared that her Grandma always had an open door, her actions and ways permeating not just her life, but those who have been taught and loved by her. Her sacrifices, what she has lost in order for her children and grandchildren to gain, are the blessings which Ashleigh bears. When they cook together, sit together, be together, they are present to each other in love. This is what Ashleigh hopes to ritualise for her children, nieces, and nephews in the years to come. Perhaps you might like to take some time to reflect on how we got to this point in our reflection; there are some questions at the end of the reflection that may be helpful.

✻ ✻ ✻

The shouting of children.
The taste of bread shared.
The ponderings of what is not said.

While we were contemplating the simple moments of children shouting, bread being shared and ponderings not said we were holding the 80,000-year-old stories that Jen, Tamilyn and Ashleigh's ancestors have kept alive: the words communicated through telepathy and intuitiveness; oral and written stories shared in different ways. These words have their own spirit and sense of presence that has allowed them to live on through our lives.

As we were preparing this reflection, Jen felt the presence of all the young women who she has worked with at St Monica's College. Those from the Islands, the Cape, the Tableland; their wisdom and ways. Rachel and Jen got teary as they heard Tamilyn and Ashleigh talk about their connection to country, the importance of listening deeply to the wisdom of their elders and the responsibility they have to share First Nations Knowings and Culture with the younger students they are role models for.

What we thought we would end up unpacking, was not to be. We listened deeply to ancestors who have animated the Christian tradition in new ways.

In this deep listening, it was not just that our ears that were attuned, it was that our whole bodies were attuned to the fullness of the world around us. We became aware, fully aware of each other and the spirit. There was a stillness. A wholeness.

Perhaps this is what Jesus sensed on his journey into Jerusalem, towards his death. A stillness. Moments of acute awareness. Knowledge of the presence of the Spirit.

Perhaps this too, is what your experience of Holy Week could be. Still. Aware. In the company of the Spirit.

## QUESTIONS FOR REFLECTION

- What did Jesus hear when the children cheered and shouted at him as he entered Jerusalem?
- What would Jesus say if he knew that today, children from this country had lost their stories because of decisions made by those in power not so long ago?
- Who made the bread which was served to Jesus on the night of the Last Supper?
- What did the bread taste like and did the one who baked it, knead it with love?
- What will you bring to the table and who will share in the meal?
- How can you be still?
- How can you welcome the presence of the Spirit in your life?

## NOTES

1. Yunkaporta T and Shillingsworth D, 'Relationally Responsive Standpoint', *Journal of Indigenous Research*, 2020, 8(4), https://digitalcommons.usu.edu/kicjir/vol8/iss2020/4.
2. *St Pauls Sunday Missal*, St Pauls Publication, Strathfield, 2011.
3. Byrne B SJ, *The Hospitality of God: A reading of Luke's Gospel*, St Pauls Publications, Strathfield, 2015, p 188.

# Celebration
## Mark 16:15–20

### ELIZABETH YOUNG

A couple of years ago, Sr Regina Wamp SND showed me around a HIV/AIDS centre, which she managed deep in the highlands of Papua New Guinea (PNG).

Then last year, she shared that, although Covid had not spread far in the country, and was not in their area, it had caused the centre to close. Six of their patients had died because they were unable to get the care and medical support they needed. People were dying due to the invisible reach of Covid, especially those least able to adapt to Covid measures – the marginalised, the colonised, and the vulnerable.

This story is almost the opposite, the negative example of our gospel from Mark for the Feast of the Ascension. Like Covid, Jesus' presence extends far beyond his physical reach, causing reactions that could scarcely be imagined.

In the gospel, we hear how Jesus sends his disciples out to proclaim the Good News to all creation, to cast out devils, to speak in every language and to heal. Jesus is to be taken into heaven, but his work is to live on through them. They will no longer see him physically, but they know he is present through his signs – life, hope, joy and unity.

Mark doesn't include the dramatic details of Luke's scene. There is no cloud, staring disciples or explanatory angels, which figure in most artworks of the Ascension. But this Ascension story adds to Mark's original gospel, with pieces spliced together from other Resurrection narratives.

Under this writer's hand, the details do not matter. Jesus is simply taken to heaven with God and his disciples immediately go and share his message by word and deed. There is not even a Pentecost; Jesus' parting words are enough.

But the Ascension moment is important for Christians and helps us to share Jesus' message beyond our own boundaries. There must have been some transition from Jesus' resurrection to the work of Christian witnessing. Somehow, he had to leave that form of his presence – as our experience of Jesus now is different from the experience of him in his bodily form.

This transition, which we have labelled the Ascension, is part of the Paschal Mystery, a part that is often forgotten or overshadowed. To understand it better, I revisited *The Eternal Year* by Karl Rahner, one of the greatest theological minds of the last century. He shares beautiful meditations on the mysteries of our faith through the liturgical cycle.

Writing about Good Friday, Rahner reflects, 'In death [Christ] has become the heart of this earthly world, the divine heart of the innermost heart of the world.'[1] Because Jesus died, he belongs all the more to the earth – his 'descent' was to the womb, the heart, the unity of creation. I find that gives a bit of depth to our Profession of Faith, when we say, 'he descended into hell'.

Rahner goes on to describe Christ's resurrection as beginning to transform the world into himself. As Christ has risen in his body, he has raised and accepted all of creation along with him. That is why, Rahner says, as children of the earth, we must love the earth, as Christ did.[2] What an insight! Our faith is not just about getting to heaven, but following Christ to embrace and transform this earth, right here and now. Equally, what a responsibility!

Finally, Rahner meditates on the Ascension. He discovers the radical value of the Incarnation: Christ became matter, and then in ascending, he took that matter with him to heaven. He says that 'Because [Christ] wanted to come close to us definitively, he has gone away and has taken us with him.'[3]

So Rahner explains that in some way, we are already in God, as God is permanently in us, within creation, through the Spirit. Creation, Incarnation, Passion, Resurrection, Ascension and Pentecost have together realised the infinite relationship between the Creator and the creation. And that is definitely Good News.

This might seem very airy-fairy, poetical but theoretical. I might be accused of being disconnected with reality, with Covid, HIV/AIDS and so much other human and non-human suffering. How is Christ more present among us today? And how do we act differently because of the Ascension?

Now I am definitely not a scientist – I didn't take after my Mum at all. But my little sister followed her into chemistry. I spoke with her about Jesus' Ascension and asked if there were any scientific process that might illustrate it in some way. She described sublimation to me.

You might have seen it for yourself at a theatre where dry ice becomes a fog or a smoke that creates an eerie mood and then dissipates away for the next scene. This process is actually the sublimation of carbon dioxide, which, unlike water, goes from solid to gas without any liquid state. As a solid, it is dense and small and cold, but when released from its freezing conditions, it quickly occupies the whole space as a gas. A small amount can fill a room, and without enough ventilation, it can replace all the oxygen.

So, we might say, Christ is now among us, not as a small, humanoid solid that we can see and touch, but infiltrating every corner of the universe in a way we cannot see. And if we know that Christ is present, through the Spirit, like the colourless, odorless gas, we can recognise the signs, or the effects that Christ has.

Christ's presence can replace all that is not of God in our universe. We are all now in God, as God is in us – reconciling all things to Godself. Of course, the parable only goes so far – the resurrected Christ is not dissipating smoke, but sublimation does illustrate how he can be more present though no longer seen.

And Christ is present not in some vague, foggy way, but in the cries of the earth and the cries of the poor, through our sacramental life, and through the hands and feet, the paws and tendrils of every creature that does his work.

In Matthew's Gospel, we hear how our service to the vulnerable is a service to Christ himself. Jesus also says, 'This is my body', 'This is my blood'[4] and 'where two or three are gathered in my name, I am there among them.'[5] And St Paul reminds us: 'Do you not realise that

Jesus Christ is in you?'⁶ Christ's ongoing presence is revealed in the signs of love, of healing, of nourishment, of reconciliation, of raising up creatures to something better. It is Christ's work and therefore it is our work. This is the Good News we proclaim, through words and deeds of healing, peace, justice and ecology.

Our faith is about action: it is about loving the world and loving it enough to change it for the better. It is being present to Christ through the sacraments, yes, but also about being his sacraments to channel his grace abroad. Our faith is recognising suffering, and the interconnectedness of suffering, and the call to further God's mission and reign by relieving that suffering.

Because Christ has ascended, Christ lives through every tear and every hand that wipes the tear away. The signs that accompany God's word and sacramental action confirm what we believe. And we have a responsibility to proclaim this to all creation.

In March 2021, Sr Regina graduated with a Diploma in Pastoral Ministry, along with eighteen other consecrated Sisters born in PNG. This moment of progress, of education and women's leadership is a sign of Christ's presence. For the first time, women have had theology classes at the same level as the men, and it has proved that leadership in faith and good works go together.

Sr Regina continues to work with those living with HIV/AIDS, but she does so as an educated religious leader, who represents the care and mercy of our God who rose, ascended and lives in us. So may we also share this Good News in our words and works today. Let us not wait for a sign, let us be the sign.

## NOTES

1. Rahner K, *The Eternal Year* (J Shea trans), Burns & Oates, London, 1964, p 91.
2. *Ibid.*, p 93.
3. *Ibid.*, p 104.
4. Matt 26:26, 27.
5. Matt 18:20.
6. 2 Cor 13:5.

**CELEBRATION**
**ASCENSION C**

# Empty Cross, Empty Tomb and Empty Space
### Luke 24:46–53

PATRICIA THERESE BENEDICT THOMAS

In Acts 1:1–11 we are reminded that in all the stuff of life, we have the Spirit within and around us. When Jesus ascended, he made way for us to feel the power of the Spirit and do 'even greater works'. Jesus ascending to heaven is not an act of abandonment, but one of empowerment and transformation in relationships.

Jesus says: 'You will receive power when the Holy Spirit has come upon you; and you will be my witnesses' (v.8a).

Commentators on Vatican II's pastoral constitution on the 'Church in the Modern World' (*Vatican II Gaudium et Spes*) remind us:

> We are not called to abandon the world but to remain in it and to take responsibility for its well ordering. The paschal mystery is a challenge to us to lift the world to the heavens.[1]

As people who belong to a global Church, our task is 'to uncover, cherish, and ennoble all that is true, good, and beautiful in the human community'.

In Luke 24:50–53 '... while he was blessing them, he withdrew from them and was carried up into heaven', we are reminded that – at times – only by someone's going away, can others receive the full blessing of that person's spirit and discover that same divine spirit within them.

The pain of letting go of a friend or family member is often excruciating. Once a loved one has passed through death, we may feel overwhelmed with a sense of being orphaned, abandoned, or of losing a vital life-connection. Yet later we may feel their presence in a deeper and purer way, and experience gratitude for their lives.

This comes at a cost, and that cost is grief. Through, with, and in Christ, we live our own and each other's paschal mysteries. What happens to Christ happens to us. In John 16:7, when Jesus was preparing to leave this earth, he kept repeating the words:

> Still, I am telling you the truth. It is for your own good that I am going, because unless I go, the Paraclete [Holy Spirit] will not come to you; but if I go, I will send him to you.[2]

Rather than say that grief is the price of love: grief is a form of love, an act of love, and, at times, the absence of that love. Through grief, the Spirit leads us vulnerable, in the face of death, through love to hope. All of us experience our own ascensions and that of others. It's all part of letting God do for us, what we cannot do for ourselves – giving us NEW LIFE and NEW SPIRIT in all our relationships. Jesus shows us that our lives can only be fully received after we ascend.

An empty cross, an empty tomb, an empty space allows the Spirit to descend upon us all.

Grief has no timeline. Death does not end our stories; death does not end our relationships. Jesus' paschal mystery is the blueprint for our own. And God is with us in living our grieving. There is no vision of a God – Father, Son and Spirit – or our family and friends, who have gone through death, somewhere else apart from us. If we do not see God in our experience of all this, there is nowhere else to see God.

Christ lives, suffers, dies, rises, and ascends amongst us.

Of all the movements within the paschal mystery, the Ascension is the least understood. Fr Ron Rolheiser opens up a refreshed theology and spirituality of the Ascension, explaining how to manage our own ascensions, and acknowledge painful goodbyes: in other words, grief.[3]

For the first disciples, the forty days between the Resurrection and the Ascension were not a time of unadulterated joy. Rather it was a time of some joy, but also of considerable confusion, despondency, and loss of faith.

In the days before the Ascension, the disciples were overjoyed whenever they recognised again their risen Lord. Yet most of the time they were confused, despondent, and full of doubt because they were unable to recognise the new presence of Christ in what was happening around them.

Eventually they grasped the fact that something had died, but that something else, far richer, had been born, and that now they needed to give up clinging to the way Jesus had formerly been present to them, so that he could be present to them in a new way. The main point is to refuse to cling to what once was, let it go, so that you can now recognise the new life you are already living, and receive its spirit.

The synoptic gospels teach this to us in their images of the Ascension, where a bodily Jesus blesses everyone and then rises physically out of their sight. John 20:17a gives us the same theology, but in a different picture. He does this in his description of the encounter on Easter morning between Jesus and Mary Magdalene when Jesus says, 'Do not hold on to me because I have not yet ascended to the Father.'

The Church today is in that time between the Resurrection and the Ascension, feeling considerable despondency, with its imagination attuned to a former understanding of Christ, unable to recognise Christ clearly in the present moment, or in the complex, diverse world we all inhabit. For many of us today, to live in faith is to be in that time between the death of Christ and the Ascension, vacillating between joy and despondency, refusing to cling, so we can ascend beyond the old life.

Rolheiser suggests that on the road of faith, there's bad news and good news.[4] The bad news is that invariably our understanding of Christ gets crucified. The good news is that Christ is always very much alive, present to us still, and in a deeper way. The Ascension names and highlights a paradox that lies deep at the centre of life, namely, that we all reach a point in life where we can only give our presence more deeply by going away so that others can receive the full blessing of our spirits.

What does that mean? Why is it better sometimes that we go away?

The paradox of love and intimacy means that to remain present to someone we love, we must sometimes be absent. We can only fully bless each other when we go away. That is why most of us only 'get' the blessing our loved ones and not-so-loved ones, were for us, after they die.

That is part of the mystery of love. Eventually we all reach a point where what is best for everyone is that we go away so that we can leave our spirit behind. The gift that our lives are can only be fully received after we ascend.

The Ascension was the final stage of Jesus' human life and every human life, when the material world is reunited to its spiritual Source – eternal life. The Ascension of Jesus does not signal his departure from our midst. It points to a new mode of presence, that is ours for the taking too, that will endure until we all meet again together.

Through, with, and in Christ Jesus' Passion and death – the loss of life, his Resurrection – the reception of new life, we find Ascension: the refusal to cling, as ascending beyond the old life. We grieve and are ready for Pentecost – the reception of new Spirit, for the new eternal life. When we stop clinging, when we give ourselves, our family, and friends over to God in trust, new life will be conceived, and that new Spirit will be released.

Grant, we pray, God, that we who believe that your Only Begotten Son, our Redeemer, ascended this day to the heavens, may in spirit dwell in the heavenly realms. Who lives and reigns with the unity of the Holy Spirit, one God, for ever and ever.

Amen

## NOTE

1. https://www.vatican.va/archive/hlst._councils/ii_vatican_councll/documents/vat·li_const_ 19651207 _gaudium-et-spes_en html
2. John 16:7, *New Jerusalem Bible.*
3. https://ronrolheiser.com/managing-an-ascension-2/#.Y5qvZnZBxPY
4. https://ronrolheiser.com/painful-goodbyes-and-the-ascension/#.Y5qvznZBxPY

**CELEBRATION**
**PENTECOST**

# Trinity, Pentecost and Climate Change
### The Theology of Life
### John 15:26–27, 16:12–15

DI RAYSON

## Introduction

The readings for Pentecost include the Gospel of John chapters 15 and 16, complemented by the narrative of Pentecost in Acts chapter 2. These readings connect theological concepts of God as Trinity: God who exists in three forms as Creator, Redeemer, and Advocate. John 15:1–11 already introduces a key idea: that of being in relationship, or 'relationality'. Jesus teaches that he is the vine that disciples are to abide in. We, the branches, abide in the vine who is Christ, tended by the vine grower, Almighty God (see John 15:5).

Jesus is preparing the disciples to be ready for the coming of the Spirit. Jesus describes his Spirit as παράκλητος, 'advocate', 'helper', or 'comforter' (John 15:26) as the Spirit of truth, one who will guide the church and enable the church to speak, testifying to Christ (v.26).

Pentecost (Acts 2) ushers in the transition from God being present in the human form of Jesus, to God dwelling with us in Spirit, and empowering the church community to preach the gospel. These readings present a dense theological moment in the New Testament.

In this piece, I will simply highlight several aspects of Pentecost that might help us negotiate the world in which we find ourselves. It is a world that remains in the grip of pandemic, a world poisoned with vitriolic intolerance and gripped by self-justification, and a world facing the existential crisis of climate change.

Perhaps, like me, you are wearying of the succession of crises that we have faced over the past several years. Where I live in rural New South Wales, I have faced a terrible drought that turned the soil to grey dust and dried the waterways to stone. We suffered the record-breaking bushfires that blazed through much of this land we now call Australia, turning our skies blood red and then black as people huddled at the water's edge for escape. We faced hailstorms, mouse plagues, and repeated floods, as people are still homeless from the Black Winter and Summer of 2019–20. Through all of this we have faced the COVID-19 pandemic that has destabilised what we came to think of as normal life.

As tragic as the human cost has been through each of these disasters, the mortality of our fellow species has been so much worse. An estimated three billion creatures died in those horrific bushfires, with some species pushed to the precipice of extinction (AIDR, n.d.).[1] Hundreds of livestock were drowned in my local area alone in the first of the series of floods from the extended *La Niña*. We've seen massive fish kills in our suffocating rivers and the repeated bleaching and death of our beloved Great Barrier Reef. We know that the propensity for animal viruses to crossover to humans is increasing with habitat loss and climate change and so new illnesses like COVID-19 will be more common as the world heats (IPCC 2001). While we might be weary of these events, we can also interrogate and understand them theologically. Pentecost, as an expression of Trinity, helps to do that.

## Doctrine of Trinity

We can think about the Trinity of God as being the ultimate image of interdependence and relationality: the three aspects of God in a total communion of love for each other and enabling the others to fulfil their roles. In traditional language, we could say that God the 'Son' exists as Son precisely because there is a 'Father'. Similarly, God who redeems the world can only do so because God is also creator. It is God's world to redeem. God who comes as Spirit to energise and sustain, sustains that which is created by the 'Father' and redeemed by the 'Son'. While many of us shun patriarchal references to God, what supersedes such labels is a picture of the three persons of the Trinity fulfilling roles in cooperation and in doing so, complementing each other. God is Creator, Redeemer, and Sanctifier, continuously loving and sustaining in perfect unity.

God as Trinity is a foundational theological doctrine to what is known as *imago Dei* (the image of God). If we understand ourselves to be created in the image of God, and God is in relationship with God's self and creation, then this means that we are also created to be in relationship with God and with each other. Furthermore, this reciprocal nature of relationships is imaged throughout the entire biosphere. All of creation is created in relationships. The science of ecology identifies and describes the network of relationships throughout life on Earth and the Earth System that sustains it. Ecology is from the same root as economy and ecumenism: οιχοσ, the household. Creation is one household of interrelationships, imaging God who is one.

The prayer of Colossians 1:15–20 teaches us that Christ, the first born of creation, is in and through all things, and that through Christ the whole of creation holds together (vv.15–17). It is for this reason that I am so interested in how we, as a church, respond to the demands of climate change. We know that we are created in the image of God to be in relationship with the rest of creation. The science of ecology tells us that the very nature of creation is interdependent and interrelational.

It helps to have a theological underpinning in considering responses to the increasing weather events and pandemics associated with climate, and how we might work in our church-communities to both support the victims, challenge the causes, hold governments accountable, and 'seize the wheel itself,' following Dietrich Bonhoeffer (Bonhoeffer [1933] 2009, 365).[2]

## From Babel to Pentecost

An aspect of biblical theology is considering how the Bible 'speaks to itself'. What I mean is how messages from the past from the Hebrew Bible have resonance in the stories of the New Testament, and in turn speak into our own present. When we imagine the disciples at Pentecost with tongues of flames on their heads, we remember God as

Spirit in a tower of flame guiding the Hebrews through the desert at night out of Egypt and into freedom. In the same way, the Spirit who comes at Pentecost guides the expanded people of God out of slavery – from legalism, hierarchy, and exclusivity. The Spirit advocates and helps us to speak truth to power, guiding the church to a type of freedom that exists for the benefit of others.

Remember the story of the tower of Babel? At the start of Genesis 11, the whole world had one language and a common speech. In their hubris, the people made a tower so that they could make a name for themselves. God confused their language to thwart this plan and to stifle their pride. The people were scattered.

Pentecost is a reversal of the Babel story, or a fulfilment of it. At Pentecost, while the disciples are waiting on God, with the sound of rushing wind fire descends, divides, and rests on each of their heads. They are filled with the Holy Spirit and begin to speak in other languages. Everyone can hear their words of praise in their own language. The confusion of sin is replaced with the clarity of the gospel. Babel is undone by Pentecost.

Peter quotes the prophet Joel (2:28) that:

> ...your sons and your daughters shall prophesy, and your young men shall see visions, and your old men shall dream dreams. Even upon my slaves, both men and women, in those days I will pour out my Spirit; and they shall prophesy.
>
> And I will show portents in the heaven above and signs on the earth below, blood, and fire, and smoky mist. (Acts 2:17b–19)

The Earth has never before experienced the trauma of human-induced climate change and we suffer. We are the cause of suffering and even extinction to our fellow species. And yet, the Spirit who comes to us at Pentecost is our advocate. The spirit allows us to speak truth, to speak with clarity, and bring words of healing.

The prophet Joel pre-figures the time when women will prophesy and speak truth to power. That time is now. We are those women, filled with the Spirit of God to bring healing to our land and to all species who dwell within it. As we experience Pentecost, year after year, I pray that you might dwell on your own role in speaking truth to power and to bring healing and soothing to the world. This truly is salvation.

## REFERENCES

Australian Institute for Disaster Resilience (AIDR) (n.d.) New South Wales, July 2019–March 2020. 'Bushfires – Black Summer', Australian Government, https://knowledge.aidr.org.au/resources/black-summer-bushfires-nsw-2019-20/, accessed 7 September 2022.

Bonhoeffer D, *Dietrich Bonhoeffer Works, vol. 12: Berlin: 1932–1933*, Fortress Press,Min, USA, 2009.

'Working Group II Report to the Assessment Report III', IPCC, Geneva International Panel on Climate Change (IPCC), 2001.

**CELEBRATION**
**FEAST OF ST MARY OF THE CROSS MACKILLOP**

# St Mary of the Cross MacKillop
## Matthew 6:25–34

### ANGELA MARQUIS

One cold Italian morning, as I travelled through Europe with a guitar and little else, I rested on a park bench beneath a beautiful, expansive tree. I'd spent the night walking the streets and was feeling cold, hungry, and a little desperate. Suddenly, the tree above me came to life with colour, movement and sound. The roosting birds were waking, chattering to each other, flapping their wings excitedly to get warm, and hopping from branch to branch. I was entranced. My desolate thoughts faded as I realised I was no longer alone. I gazed in wonder at their joyous movement, as the dawn rays sparkled off the leaves and the warming sun rose silently to greet us.

The gospel for the Feast of St Mary of the Cross MacKillop always transports me back to this moment of awakening, a moment of awe and complete trust that all will be well. These creatures knew the night was almost over, they felt the rhythm of life and lacked my anxiety for warmth and food.

I wonder why this gospel passage was chosen for such a courageous Australian woman and her all-consuming faith. Perhaps because Mary MacKillop clothed the impoverished children she taught, and fed the hungry and destitute mothers and women in her refuges? Or does it portray her utter reliance upon God's providence?

'Do not worry' instructs Jesus (v.25). Do not worry about what you might wear, what you might eat, what you might say (v.31). Indeed, the Matthean Jesus assures us that God will constantly provide.

This statement bothers me.

If God worries about us more than the lilies in the fields, clothed more gloriously than Solomon, yet thrown in the fire tomorrow (v.30), why are so many people homeless and cold? If we are of more value than the nourished birds of the air (v.26), why do so many of us starve? We are invited to reflect upon the beauty of the flowers and grasses, to contemplate the birds, then consider how much more we are worth than these two life forms – a point that often becomes our focus. Yet, Jesus is not oblivious to the plight of the poor, nor is he fostering human authority.

When we focus upon our own worth, our own superiority over other creatures, our dominion over and above one another, we fail to see as God sees, we fail to act as God acts. In asking us to recognise the beauty of the grass and birds, Jesus is not assuring us of our own importance but crucially, reminding us that God cares for all these things as well as us. All lifeforms are cared for by God, thus we too are cared for by God. Perhaps Jesus' request is articulated more clearly by Job (12:7) who says, 'Ask the animals and they will teach you,' fleshed out beautifully by Elizabeth Johnson: '...speak to the birds of the air, the plants of the earth, and the fish of the sea and they will instruct you.'[1] The question is, will we listen?

I wonder whether the seed of this gospel is derived from the first Beatitude – Blessed are the poor in Spirit (Matt. 5:1). Blessed are those who recognise their total dependence upon God, who allow God to pervade their being, who do not worry what they might eat or wear or say or do, for when the time comes, God's presence will be revealed. Those who are poor in spirit recognise the nearness of God. They've simplified their lives, emptied themselves of self.

Mary MacKillop embodied such simplicity. Not the silent, subservient model of feminine, saintly piety that has often been endorsed by the Catholic Church – the veneration of blended virginity and motherhood that gazes down in silent judgement from countless statues and artworks, rather, the simplicity found in her embodiment of deep peace as she endured the trials of her life. Mary stood up for what she held most dear and forged difficult paths in extreme circumstances.

Mary's work in the world was deeply suffused with a sense of the sacred in the everyday. She challenged and disrupted the dominant rule she lived under and instead, shed light upon injustice, speaking for the silenced and oppressed, illuminating the narrow-mindedness of those who sought to control her. She dealt with the harshness of her environment and humanity in all its forms and guises, never wavering in her conviction that her trials seemed to her to be the will of God. Amidst raging storms, her heart remained calm.

Excommunicated on the 22nd of September 1871, Mary wrote about her experience of kneeling at the feet of the bishop:

> I really felt like one in a dream. I seemed not to realise the presence of the bishop and priests. I know I did not see them; but I felt, oh, such a love for their office, a love, a sort of reverence for the very sentence which I then knew was being in full force passed upon me. I do not know how to describe the feeling, but I was intensely happy and felt nearer to God than I had ever felt before.[2]

While a first reading of her words may situate Mary's experience firmly within the submissive stereotype of the female saint, Kathleen McPhillips[3] understands this utter closeness to God in suffering to be an expression of Mary's unwritten hagiography, a life unfettered by patriarchal expectations that female saints remain within the bounds of femininity and passivity. Mary 'actively meets God through her body...revealing the presence of a divine Other...it is her body, her flesh and pain that imparts the word of God.'[4] Mary, like Jesus silent before Pilate, knew in her heart that the bishop 'had no power over [her] unless it had been given [to] him from above' (John 19:11). Indeed, Bishop Sheil lamented his decision and, on his death bed five months later, he lifted her sentence. The experience of deep pain, silencing and exclusion at the hands of the Church did not subdue Mary. Like the birds, Mary would not be silenced.

This Gospel characterises the life of Mary of the Cross not purely because of her complete trust in God's will, but her faith to endure when those who thought themselves of more worth, either ignored her or sought to discredit her. How often do we silence those in our midst whom we judge less important than ourselves? How different was Mary's experience from that of women in the Church today? For how long must women kneel, with eyes cast down, and obediently accept the law of the fathers? Women's bodies, their flesh and pain, also impart the word of God. Yet, the rules, traditions and rituals of our faith often allow us to condemn, deprive and ignore others, because we are unable to love as God loves.

In 2002, possessing only the clothes on my back, the peace in my heart was such that the mere sound of the birds in a leafy canopy calmed my soul. Twenty years on, with a comparative abundance of food and clothing, birdsong at dawn rarely has the same effect. Yet, when I fail to hear the birds welcoming the new day, when I disregard the colour of the flowers or the dance of the fields in the breeze, I am failing to love as God loves.

Christ calls us to be wholly present to life. To awaken like the birds and proclaim the rising sun. Furthermore, we are summoned to stand, alongside St Mary of the Cross MacKillop, and speak, to refuse to be silent. To be truly poor in spirit, we can only trust in a God whose flourishing life force animates the grass and flowers, and rides the thermals alongside the winged creatures of the air. A God who is proclaimed from the rooftops, the trees and the lecterns, unfettered by human form.

## NOTES

1. Johnson EA, *Ask the beasts: Darwin and the God of love*, Bloomsbury, London, 2014, xv.
2. Gardiner P, *Mary MacKillop: An extraordinary Australian*, Edgecliff: Sisters of St Joseph, 1993, p 105.
3. McPhillips K, Post-modern sainthood' 'Hearing the voice of the saint' and the uses of feminist hagiography, *Women Scholars of Religion and Theology 3*, 2003, pp 1–22.
4. *Ibid.,* p 16.

**CELEBRATION**
**CHRIST THE KING**

# On the Side of Truth
## John 18:33–37

DI LANGHAM

'Are you the King of the Jews?' Pilate asks. Pilate was looking at Jesus with his Roman eyes. His questions seem to ask whether He is a king. Pilate has no understanding of Jesus' answers. Jesus says, 'My kingdom is not of this world.' Pilate doesn't get it. He is looking at the physical situation, not the spiritual.

The lens that Pilate looks through is the lens of a Roman official. When we look at the Jewish leaders, we see the lens that they are using is one that is concerned with keeping their boundaries, laws, and power. So, we have two lenses, Roman and Jewish.

When I read this, I cannot help but think that we look at our worldviews through lens as well. And that includes me. I look at the world and the church through Indigenous eyes. I look at our history and see the lens of the colonists including the church and its effects on our people.

So, what was a king in our history? The colonists made and appointed kings amongst our people. They were given brass plates that were hung around their necks. The colonists used these kings to deal with communities. The Russian explorers saw this when they came to Australia and commented on it as being rather odd. It was a gesture so that the appointed kings could report between the colonial government and the Aboriginal community.

The colonial government had no idea of the power these elders had in their communities. The government did not realise that our communities are matriarchal, not patriarchal. The lens was that of the English society. I believe that the early invaders used this tool so that they didn't have to take responsibility for the taking of the land, because they used these men to help their cause.

I can see the analogy with Pilate. He did not want to have to make a decision with Jesus. He wanted to play games with the language.

Let's talk about our history while I have this chance. Let's get back to Aboriginal kings. King Billy was an Aboriginal elder. He was a Wiradjuri warrior. Wiradjuri lands boundaries probably ran south from Condobolin in New South Wales, including Wagga and Cootamundra, east to Gundagai and west along Billabong Creek totalling an area of 97,100 square kilometres. He was given a breastplate so that he then became the negotiator to the colonists concerning the lands and community decisions. King Billy was a great leader. He was very troubled with how his people were being treated. Aboriginal people were still being massacred and poisoned and their land removed. He decided to use his white man's given authority to walk from Tumut to Canberra when the First Parliament House was being opened in 1927 to speak up on behalf of his people. He was refused entry. It was reported in the local paper that he wanted to present his sovereign rights to the Federal Territory. The police tried to remove him, claiming that he and his friend John Noble were inappropriately dressed. Another lens! What you wear represents your authority. Remember Jesus and the robe and the crown of thorns.

This protest was the forerunner of many protests and court actions concerning Land Rights and Indigenous Rights. We are still fighting those battles. King Billy thought that he had the same authority. The sad and devastating part of all this was he was not respected or listened to. King Billy had the history and authority of 60,000 years of his ancestral knowledge and spirituality. He was grounded in this land. Those men at Parliament house had no idea of the wealth of King Billy.

That is what happened with Jesus and Pilate in their conversation. Jesus was not respected or listened to. Jesus was talking about a kingdom that Pilate and the Jewish leaders had no idea about.

I take great pride in King Billy's story. It gives me the courage to share our story.

I remember when I was invited to do an Acknowledgement of Country in the Newcastle Anglican Cathedral many years ago. The Cathedral is built near the community campsite of the Awabakal people. So there would have been corroborees, celebrations, dancing and singing in that area for at least 40,000 years. For that reason, I decided to tell the Newcastle story or *Muloobinba*. It is the story of the Giant Kangaroo.

There was a giant kangaroo, who was selfish and lustful, and putting desire before his code of behaviour, attacked a female wallaby. Such an act was in conflict with the laws of kinship and preservation of bloodlines. It destroyed the totemic structure.

After the attack, herds of wallabies gave chase to the perpetrator, who fled over hills and through the bush, heading for Muloobinba. Though he could leap further than the wallabies, he knew that it was inevitable that he would be caught and killed because he had reached the sea. But as he reached the sea, a mist intervened and he was lost to the sight of his pursuers. He took advantage of this and swam to Nobby's Island and entered the island and hid himself.

The wallabies gave up the chase, believing the sea had claimed the Kangaroo. But according to tradition, the kangaroo was never sure of his safety. So now and then, he would jump up and down, which would cause the cliff to tremble and the cliffs to crumble as a warning to the wallabies to not get too close. That's why we have earthquakes.

I told this story because, for one thing, the cathedral had major damage in the Newcastle earthquake. The other reason was that the cathedral is not 200 years old, but the Awabakal story is thousands of years old. The spirituality of the earth underneath it is priceless.

This story did not fit with the audience that I shared it with. I received a letter questioning the conflict of this spirituality with the Christian story. It was a classic case of looking at Australian spirituality through the lens of the English church. I call it 'pot-plant church'. Instead of listening to the spirituality of the land, the Church comes in a pot plant and sits on top of the land. What a wealth of spirituality it loses by doing that.

As part of the Mass, I had a didgeridoo playing during the Eucharist. I was also questioned about this instrument being used. My answer was when I look up at the walls of the Cathedral I see sets of pipes, through which wind is blown to make sound that is pleasing to the soul. What is a didgeridoo but a pipe through which wind is blown? What is the difference? No one had an answer.

I think that Pilate and the Jewish leaders were looking at Jesus through their own worldviews. The lens was their secular teaching, laws and rituals. They could not see the spiritual world that Jesus was alluding to. They just did not understand.

Both Pilate and the Jewish leaders saw kings as powerful and wealthy. Kings have everything they need. To get where they want to go, they build up their own wealth. They take from the poor and build up their wealth. They really had no understanding of who Jesus was.

Jesus was King. Pilate was right. But he was a king of a kingdom that neither Pilate nor the Jewish leaders had any idea of what it looked like. Just as King Billy was a king of a culture that colonists had no idea of, the oldest living culture in the world.

Jesus answered, 'Everyone on the side of truth listens to me.'[1]

We all need to be on the side of truth. Truth and truth-telling will set us free. Truth-telling needs to happen in this land so that a true history is told. Our Indigenous story needs to be told and heard.

It's time to change our lenses.

In the name of the Father, Son and Holy Spirit. Amen.

---

### NOTE

1. John 18:37, *New International Reader's Version*, NIRV.

# Meet the Authors

**BRYNE, MOIRA**
Dr Moira Byrne grew up in rural South Australia. She moved to Adelaide after high school and joined a Catholic youth group where she met Matthew, whom she later married. In 2001, they moved to Canberra with their two very small children. Two more were welcomed in Canberra so they now have four young adult children. In 2012 she completed a PhD in political science at Australian National University (ANU), which examined religious organisations as interest groups in refugee policy. As part of the Young Catholic Women's Interfaith Fellowship, she completed a Postgraduate Diploma of Theology in 2016. Inspired by the charism of the Sisters of St Joseph, and the spiritualities of the Missionaries of the Sacred Heart and the Good Samaritan sisters, Moira is thankful for the individuals and groups who have shaped her experience of God and faith. Moira is an accomplished writer with many publications in a variety of places, as well as a few prizes. She has qualifications in policy, education and economics, and has also studied law, Italian language, and literature. She is also a graduate of the Australian Institute of Company Directors and an Accredited Editor. Moira works as a federal public servant but occasionally dabbles in academia.

**COLOE, MARY**
Dr Mary Coloe is a Presentation sister and a professor of New Testament at Yarra Theological Union, a college within the University of Divinity, Melbourne. Her primary focus in teaching and writing is the Gospel of John. Her two-volume commentary on John in the Wisdom Commentary Series was published in 2021. This series is a feminist commentary on the biblical books. The commentary will be available through Garratt Publishing and Pauline Books and Media. She also has three small books of reflections on each Sunday Gospel of the year: *Sundays under the Southern Cross* – available through Garratt Publishing. Mary has taught at Australian Catholic University and a number of places overseas: Berkeley, California; Boston College, and Jerusalem. In recent years she has worked on an international dialogue between the Catholic Church and the Christian Church (Disciples of Christ). Mary calls this her 'Vatican hat', as this appointment was for the Pontifical Council for Christian Unity.

**CONNOLLY, MICHELE**
Dr Michele Connolly RSJ is a Sister of St Joseph Lochinvar in the Hunter Valley. She is an Associate Professor of Biblical Studies and Biblical Studies Discipline Coordinator at the Sydney College of Divinity and lectures in Biblical Studies at the Catholic Institute of Sydney, a pontifical institute of theology. After teaching in secondary schools for about ten years, she studied theology, graduating in 2008 with a PhD from Graduate Theological Union (GTU), Berkeley, California. Michele's principal area of interest is the Gospel of Mark. In 2018 her doctoral

thesis was published by T&T Clark under the title *Disorderly Women and the Order of God: An Australian Feminist Reading of the Gospel of Mark*. Michele speaks regularly around Australia at conferences on the Scriptures.

## DEAN, ANDREA

Andrea Dean has been involved in leadership, facilitation and teaching through Catholic Education in the Archdiocese of Canberra and Goulburn, the Australian Catholic University, and the University of Canberra. In 2004, she received a Churchill Fellowship and visited the United States of America to investigate programs in teacher formation. After two years as Director of the Office for the Participation of Women and Office for Lay Pastoral Ministry within the Australian Catholic Bishops Conference. Andrea now works in the community sector. She holds qualifications in education, theology, coaching, spiritual direction, and ministry. Andrea is the president of WATAC Inc. – Women and the Australian Church.

## DOHERTY, BETH

Beth Doherty is a storyteller and teacher based in Canberra, Australia. She has been involved in Church throughout her life through music ministry, the written word, education, and communications. An advocate for social justice, Beth has spent time with marginalised communities, working in Spanish-speaking South and Central America. She is a Secondary Religious Education leader in the Archdiocese of Canberra and Goulburn. Author of two books, *Tweet others as you would wish to be tweeted* (2015) and *All the beautiful things* (2020), she is completing a text for publication with Garratt to be released in 2023 titled *An Attitude of Beatitude*, which will look at social justice education and altruism.

## DUTTON, MONICA

Dr Monica Dutton is the Spirituality and Mission Animation Leader for the Sisters of the Good Samaritan, and works at the Congregational Offices in Glebe, Sydney. Monica has a background in education and has worked as a teacher, leader and consultant in primary, secondary and tertiary educational settings, and has Masters degrees in Educational Psychology and Religious Education. Monica is committed to professional learning and formation of staff, boards and leadership personnel and her doctorate focused on formation and transformation of staff through the experience of short-term cross-cultural immersion trips. Monica is the coordinator of the Sisters of the Good Samaritan Study and Mentoring (SAM) Program, which supports women students of theology to become voices and leaders in the Catholic Church. She is also a member of the National Catholic Education Commission's Faith Formation and Religious Education Standing Committee.

## DWYER, MEL

Sr Mel Dwyer FdCC made her religious profession as a Canossian Daughter of Charity on the 23rd of April 2005. Prior to entering religious life, she was a national-level javelin thrower with a dream of representing Australia at the Olympics. A volunteer mission experience in Africa helped her to discover that God's dream for her was to leave the sporting arena and serve radically in a consecrated religious life. Having finished her degree in Secondary Physical Education, Sr Melissa returned to Malawi, Africa where she completed seven years as principal of a secondary school. She has been awarded an honorary doctorate from the Australian Catholic University for her contribution to promoting access to education during her time in East Africa. Following her return to Brisbane, Sr Melissa was appointed as Delegation Leader for the Canossian Daughters of Charity in Australia in 2019 and in August 2022 she was elected to the Congregational General Council. She is currently living and serving in Rome, Italy as part of this international leadership team.

## DYBALL, FIONA

Fiona Dyball B.Mus, Grad Dip Music Therapy & Education, Grad Cert RE, MMusSt, MTS (Liturgy) is a musician, teacher, composer, conductor, writer, consultant, and liturgist based in Melbourne, Australia. She works extensively in liturgical and faith formation, and in music ministry as a cantor, presenter, facilitator, and workshop leader. Fiona is currently undertaking a PhD titled 'The Sung Responsorial Psalm in the Post-Conciliar Catholic Mass in the Archdiocese of Melbourne', which will also contribute 15 new musical settings of Responsorial Psalms. Fiona served for six years on the National Liturgical Music Council for the Australian Catholic Bishops Conference, is a current member of the National Executive of the Australian Pastoral Musicians Network, and is currently Coordinator of Liturgy, Faith and Mission at St Monica's College in Epping, Victoria. She is Music Consultant and Choir Leader at Immaculate Conception Catholic Parish in Hawthorn, Victoria and a Sessional Academic at Australian Catholic University.

## EASTWOOD, MICHELLE

Dr Michelle Eastwood is Director of Research at Australian Lutheran College and Executive Officer for the Australian and New Zealand Association of Theological Schools (ANZATS) and the Council of Deans of Theology. She has degrees in Psychology, History, Education and Theology. Her current research interests include shame, gender and sexuality, the Hebrew Bible, worship and liturgy, and public theology. Michelle is currently exploring the Women-Church journal in connection with the Australian Women in Religion project. As part of this work, she is engaging with Wikipedia as an editor, writer and critic. Michelle lives on Wauthaurong land and believes that reparations must be paid for all the damage that has been perpetrated against the First Nations of this land.

## ENGLEBRECHT, KATE

Kate Englebrecht is currently serving as a Prison Chaplain for the Catholic Diocese of Bathurst NSW. She lives in central western NSW after several years of pastoral care work in isolated, outback communities. Kate has experience in Church leadership as a Diocesan Chancellor, Director of Mission/Identity as well as years in education, chaplaincy and mission management. Her experience in pastoral care has influenced her thinking and honed her skills to listen and speak. Kate supports the work of NSW Health Palliative Care Volunteers across NSW and has a particular commitment to those who care for the dying in rural communities. Kate has tutored in Christian Spirituality at tertiary level and been a secondary teacher of senior HSC English and Studies of Religion. As an Anglican in her early life, and responding to a call to ordained ministry, Kate trained for the Anglican priesthood and became interested in Catholic life when she began to study theology. As a result of exposure to the great writers of the Spiritual Classics and her studies in Western Spirituality, she became a Catholic in the late 1980s.

## ESPINO, RACY SALVACION

Racy Espino writes: My vocation is married life. I have been happily married to my husband for 16 years and counting. We are blessed with two children, one in high school and one in primary. I was raised in a devout Catholic family in the Philippines, with 500 years of Christian history from Spain. Both my grandmothers were my role models in their faith and living life according to God's plans. My father was a former seminarian who found his calling as a family man and dedicated his life to providing lights and sound systems in Catholic churches around the Philippines. I am passionate about planting and nurturing seeds of faith in our children. When my eldest asked questions about Joseph the Dreamer, I took it upon myself to brush up my religious knowledge. I studied 'Foundations of Lay Pastoral Ministry', and started volunteering in our parish. I got so heavily involved in the implementation of the Sacraments of Initiation in our parish that I took on the role as Pastoral Coordinator for two primary schools and four churches for nearly five years. I walk with parents in their faith journey to cultivate within them a personal relationship with our Creator. I am part of the organising committee of Mother's Prayer Groups and Spirited Women (a gathering of women in the Archdiocese of Brisbane.)

## GEMMELL, PATRICIA

Patricia Gemmell is a wife, mother, grandmother and semi-retired teacher of French, Latin and Italian. Her lifelong interest in theology and spirituality finally led her to formal study and she graduated with a Masters degree in Theology in 2014. She belongs to the Grail, an international movement and community of women, founded in the Netherlands in 1921 by Jacques van Ginneken SJ.

She has recently completed 8 years' service on the National Leadership Team and is the coordinator of the International Spirituality Network. In 2016 she presented five lectures on Eco-theology and Spirituality at the Grail summer school in Portugal. A parishioner for 37 years at St Leonards, Naremburn, Patricia has been involved in a variety of ministries over the years. She is currently a lector and Extraordinary Minister of Communion (EMC), and one of the church bell ringers. In 2018 she was asked to become her community's local animator for the Plenary Council, and since then has engaged herself wholeheartedly in the Plenary Council journey.

**JOLLY, MELINDA**
Melinda Jolly is a Catholic Indigenous woman from the Cubbitch Barta Clan in the Dharawal Nation. Melinda has been married for 27 years to Alan, has four children and four grandchildren. She originally had a background in administration in Catholic schools, then went to Australian Catholic University studying Theology as a mature-aged student. She holds a Bachelor of Theology (Hons), minoring in Philosophy and History. Melinda tutored and lectured at Australian Catholic University for over 7 years in both Systematic Theology and Biblical Studies. She has an interest in the work of Edith Stein and has given papers at international conferences on Stein. Melinda is currently the Pastoral Care Coordinator at St Vincent's Private Hospital Sydney.

**LAMBERT, CATHIE**
The Reverend Dr Cathie Lambert is a Minister of the Word in the Uniting Church, has recently completed her PhD. Cathie's current research is exploring how contemporary women on the edge of the church respond to the lives and writings of the beguine mystics from the thirteenth century. Cathie is a spiritual director and is part of the teaching staff of Dayspring's Graduate Diploma in Spiritual Direction. In 2018 she published *A Mandala a Month* Workbook to help people discover the use of mandalas as a spiritual tool. Cathie lives in Margaret River, Western Australia, with her husband and two adult children.

**LANGHAM, DI**
Reverend Di Langham writes: I am Reverend Canon Auntie Di Langham, Director of Reconciliation for Anglican Diocese of Newcastle. I am also secretary of the National Aboriginal and Torres Strait islander Anglican Council. I am 72 years of age. I have been a priest in the Diocese of Newcastle for the past 21 years and was the first Aboriginal woman in this Diocese to be ordained. I was a chaplain in Corrective Services NSW for 20 years and prior to that I was a chaplain in Juvenile Justice. I am a Boandik woman and part of the Stolen Generations history of this country, now living and working in the lands of the Awabakal and Wanaruah. I am married with four children, fourteen grandchildren and

two great grandchildren. I like to weave Aboriginal spirituality into any of my talks and talk about my past experiences in any sermons I do. I was a teacher in my past life and taught in both schools and TAFE.

## LEE, ELIZABETH

Elizabeth Lee is a spiritual director, retreat facilitator, and pastoral supervisor. She works to foster human connection through deep listening among the fringes. In recent times she has had the privilege of offering pastoral care among those living with homelessness. Prior to that she had years of ministry as a Prison Chaplain. Liz originally trained as a food technologist and with a varied career as a research scientist, museum curator, health promotion community development worker and teacher of science and religious education. She holds a Master of Arts (Theology) as well a Bachelor of Science, Graduate Diploma in Education, and a Masters of Education, a Masters of Education and a Graduate Certificate in Research Methodology, and has recently commenced a PhD. Liz is a member of the Grail, and a member in association at Pitt St Uniting Church. She is married with three adult children and is a grandmother.

## LYNCH, DANIELLE ANNE

Dr Danielle Anne Lynch is a theologian, musician, and teacher, working in Brisbane. Her work in systematic theology encompasses theology, music, and song-writing, with particular interest in feminist and queer approaches. She also works in Mission, Liturgy, Religious Identity and Culture, and Religious Education. Danielle's book on music and theology *God in Sound and Silence: Music as Theology* was published in 2018. Her album 'Into Silence', a collection of original songs exploring life in all its dimensions, including spiritual and faith aspects, was released in 2020 and her Mass setting, *Mass For All Of Us*, was published in 2022.

## MCCARTHY, ANGELA

Angela McCarthy is an adjunct senior lecturer in theology at The University of Notre Dame Australia's Fremantle campus and a member of the Plenary Council of the Catholic Church in Australia. Her first degree from Sydney University included work in Biblical Studies and Fine Arts and then further studies in Theology and education from 1993 at Notre Dame. She was awarded her PhD in 2007. Since then, she has completed a further Research Masters degree in Theology in the field of Scripture, Art and Theology. Angela has published in the areas of liturgy, icons, art and theology, liturgical music, educational practice and theological aesthetics. She is the former editor of the *Australian Journal of Liturgy*, a member of the Australian Academy of Liturgy, Chairperson of the Mandorla Art Award, a member of the Chamber of Arts and Culture WA and the Fellowship of Biblical Studies, and the editor of Pastoral Liturgy. She is a wife of 48 years, mother of four and grandmother of fourteen.

## MCEWAN, TRACY

Dr Tracy McEwan is a theologian and sociologist of religion and gender affiliated with the University of Newcastle, Australia. Her writing and research interests include women in Catholicism; domestic and family violence; sexual and spiritual abuse; gender, sexuality, and women's religious experience. Tracy is the current vice-president of WATAC Inc. – Women and the Australian Church. Her recent projects include the podcast 'Australian Women Preach' which celebrates the diverse talents of woman preachers in Australia, and the International Survey of Catholic Women, a survey of more than 17,000 Catholic women from 105 countries. Tracy holds a Doctor of Philosophy (Theology) and Master of Theology from the University of Newcastle and a Bachelor of Applied Science (Mathematics) from the University of Technology Sydney (UTS).

## MCLEAN, RACHEL • KING, JENNIFER • AH KEE, TAMILYN • UNG, ASHLEIGH

Jennifer is a proud descendant of four Aboriginal clan groups, Butchella of K'gari (Fraser Island), Djiribul of Innisfail, Gugu Yimmithir of Hopevale, and Western Yalanji of Laura in Cape York. Her great-grandparents were removed or forced off their homelands and institutionalised on Yarrabah Mission, south of Cairns. An educator, communicator and collaborator, Jennifer collaborated on the podcast with Rachel McLean, Leader Formation at Catholic Education Services Cairns. Rachel works with leadership teams and staff from 30 Catholic schools in Far North Queensland in the areas of Faith Formation, Religious Education, Outreach and Reconciliation.

For the last two years, Jen and Rachel have collaborated with students and other First Nations elders to showcase and celebrate student voices with the Cairns Catholic Education Community. This collaboration draws on the wisdom and ways of First Nations peoples and invites listeners to consider how the ancient ways of First Nations peoples of Australia can enrich and extend an encounter with the scripture.

In her role as the Indigenous Liaison Officer at St Monica's Catholic College Cairns, Jennifer works closely with all students and staff to share First Nations Knowings and embed First Nations perspectives across the curriculum. Jennifer takes a holistic approach in her professional practice with the school by serving students in developing academic, social, and spiritual health. In doing so, she challenges students to reflect on their personal values, explore the champion within themselves and have confidence in their decision-making.

Tamilyn Ah Kee is a proud descendant of the Wanyurrmajay Yidinji and Kuku Yalanji people of the lands known as Cairns and Mossman. Ashleigh Ung is a proud descendant of the Wakaid and Badulgal people of Badu Island located in Zendath Kes, or the Torres Strait. These young women share the wisdom they are acquiring to honour their ancestors and be role models for young people who are coming to know themselves and the wisdom of First Nations knowings.

## MARQUIS, ANGELA

Angela Marquis is the Liturgist at St Joseph's Catholic Church in Hobart. She studied teaching after completing a BA in English and Philosophy. Her undergraduate Honours Thesis was titled *A Theopoetics of Feminist Faith*. Angela has taught in primary schools throughout Southern Tasmania and in an Indigenous Community in the Tiwi Islands, where she undertook a Graduate Certificate in Religious Education. She continued this study with the Broken Bay Institute (BBI) and completed a Master of Theology in 2021. Angela is currently studying Biblical Hebrew with the Israel Institute. The main focus of her writing is the language of Biblical texts and liturgy, with a particular focus on the silenced female voice in major Monotheistic religions. Her paper *She who was: scriptural linguistics and the absent image of God*, was recently published in *Pastoral Liturgy* [https://researchonline.nd.edu.au/pastoral-liturgy] and she is currently working on a book chapter titled, 'Rewilding the Trinity: Reimagining the anthropomorphic God', for an upcoming publication. Angela works as a chaplain in a local primary school. She enjoys rock climbing and long leisurely beach walks with her husband and four-legged daughter.

## OVEREEM, ALISON

Alison Overeem is a proud Palawa woman from South-East Tasmania who is driven by culture, family, empowerment and creating safe spaces to build hope and dignity. Alison works to raise awareness of Aboriginal culture and history and the rights of women in society. As a result, Alison was a past member of the Tasmanian Women's Council. While working in aged care at the age of 16, Alison studied for a Bachelor of Education (Early Childhood) and graduated in 1989. Alison established the Aboriginal Children's Centre at West Moonah in 1989. As Director of the Aboriginal Children's Centre from 1989 to 2013, she helped design a state-of-the-art, award-winning, culturally inclusive children's centre at Risdon Cove – a precursor to the Child and Family Centres rolled out across Tasmania in recent years. In 2013, Alison was appointed as the Leprena Manager, Uniting Aboriginal and Islander Christian Congress (UAICC Tasmania). Alison also sits on the UAICC National Executive, UnitingCare board of Australia, Uniting Church Assembly Standing Committee and various other advocacy, policy and strategic planning committees. Alison has made numerous contributions to publications and resources nationally around culturally inclusive practice models of service delivery for Aboriginal communities. She has also been involved in advocacy and policies impacting social justice movements and climate change.

## RAYSON, DI

Dr Di Rayson is a public theologian whose specialities are ecotheology and Dietrich Bonhoeffer. She periodically appears on ABC radio discussing moral and ethical issues. She is Senior Lecturer at Pacific Theological College,

Suva, Fiji where she focuses on whole-of-life theology, decolonisation, and theologies of land and sea. Di is an elected board member of the International Bonhoeffer Society – English Language Section, and is assistant editor of *The Bonhoeffer Legacy: An International Journal*. Her research focuses on the application of Bonhoeffer's theology to ecotheology and ecoethics, based on a deep relationality with all creation. Her first book, *Bonhoeffer and Climate Change: Theology and Ethics for the Anthropocene* (Lexington) was published in 2021 based on her PhD thesis, and she has edited *Education, Religion, and Ethics: A Scholarly Collection* (Springer) due in early 2023. Before theology, Di had an extensive career in public health, community development and public policy, working as a missionary in Papua New Guinea and then in Australia's Northern Territory. She also holds a Master of Public Health through her work in training village birth attendants in the Highlands of PNG. Di is a regular preacher within the Anglican Church of Australia and across other denominations.

## REDWOOD, CHRISTINE

The Reverend Dr Christine Redwood is the Lead Pastor at Seaforth Baptist Church. She is actively involved in the Baptist denomination in NSW & ACT and has served on the Assembly Council and the Public Engagement Taskforce. Christine recently completed her PhD in preaching, the Old Testament and feminist hermeneutics. In 2011 she was the preaching intern for Morling College and works there as an adjunct lecturer. Outside of work, she loves spending time with her nieces, being creative and is interested in films, theatre, writing, and most of all, communicating God's story with others.

## RÉMOND, JACQUI

Jacqui Rémond is Co-Founder of the *Laudato Si'* Movement (LSM) and currently works with the Vatican Dicastery for Integral Human Development as Co Coordinator of the Ecology Taskforce. Jacqui is a member of the Steering Board of the *Laudato Si'* Action Platform and Co-leads the Education Sector for both the Schools and Universities Working Groups. At the Australian Catholic University Jacqui is Lead Animator of Integral Ecology in the Faculty of Theology and Philosophy teaching a *Laudato Si'* inspired program in Rome and animating communities to live an Integral Ecology. Jacqui is currently undertaking doctoral research at the School of Education, Notre Dame University, Australia.

## ROBERTS, BELINDA

I am a proud Boandik woman, forever changed by the stolen generations, and as a result live on Awabakal Country. I feel deep connections to family, spirituality, faith, country and community. I am a member of the National

Aboriginal and Torres Strait Islander Anglican Council (NATSIAC). I am also a member of Nikinpa Aboriginal Women's Art Group, where I create and express myself mostly with art by painting leaves for culturally appropriate Sorry Business. As an Aboriginal woman, social justice, reciprocity, activism and truth-telling are blueprinted in my DNA.

## SUKIUMAR-WHITE, RADHIKA

The Reverend Radhika Sukumar-White has been a Minister of the Word in the Uniting Church in Australia since 2016. A second-generation Sri Lankan Tamil Australian, she grew up in Canberra before moving to Sydney to study Physiotherapy, Music and then Theology. Radhika is interested in leading dynamic and sacred worship, preaching, teaching and walking alongside individuals in their life and faith journeys. Radhika is currently serving as Ministry Team Leader at Leichhardt Uniting Church, a young, vibrant, justice-oriented community of faith in the Inner West of Sydney. She serves alongside her husband, who also serves as Chaplain at the University of Sydney.

## TAYLOR, KATECIA

Katecia (Teash) Taylor is co-pastor of St Kilda Elsternwick Baptist Church, University of Divinity student and a resident of Melbourne's inner north. Teash has spoken at conferences and events around Australia about the intersection of being part of the LGBT+ community and a person of faith. She became a feminist and a supporter of women preaching at University when she learnt that women were not allowed to speak at her university campus' largest Christian group's main Bible talks. She has been advocating for marginalised groups ever since.

## THOMAS, PATRICIA

Patricia Therese Benedict Thomas is a pastoral theologian, reflector, pragmatist, activist, Ignatian spiritual director and retreat facilitator and an Oblate of St Benedict at Jamberoo Abbey. Patricia works as a Grief Care Managing Consultant with Catholic Cemeteries & Crematoria Sydney. Grief Care is a community of qualified pastoral care practitioners, counsellors, educators and spiritual directors offering care, empathy, and compassion to families living with the impact of loss, grief, trauma, and bereavement.

## THOMSON, GEMMA

Gemma Thomson is the Dean of Mission and Catholic Identity at Iona Presentation College in Perth, Western Australia, a Catholic school in the Presentation tradition. The co-author of *Making Jesus Real 24/7*, along with other publications, she enjoys the opportunity to share her lived experience of faith with others. Gemma active role models and promotes the Presentation charism, working closely with the Nagle Education Alliance of Australia and the Presentation Society of Australia and Papua New Guinea. She is currently undertaking a Doctor of Education at the University of Notre Dame Australia. Gemma works closely with the Presentation Sisters at local, national, and international levels in the area of justice and mission and is a member of several Archdiocesan Committees pertaining to education, formation and strategy. Gemma was a member of the Fifth Plenary Council of Australia for the Archdiocese of Perth.

Riley-Jayne Carroll and Samara Spadanuda graduated from Iona Presentation College in 2022. Throughout their time at the College, Riley-Jayne and Samara made a significant contribution to the service and faith life of Iona as they modelled the Nagle family motto 'deeds not words'.

**YOUNG, ELIZABETH**

Elizabeth Young RSM was brought up on a farm in the south of South Australia. Her father was a lay preacher in the Uniting Church, and their ministers were both men and women. However, she attended St Mary MacKillop's very first school in Penola, and was received into the Catholic Church along with family members. Elizabeth valued the sacramental worldview that she encountered and was inspired by all the religious leaders in her community. From a young age, she felt called to a vocation in religious and liturgical leadership, to share the Good News of Jesus Christ. Her life took a turn through a few years of questioning her faith and completing a degree in Circus Arts. From there she discerned God's call to become a Sister of Mercy, professing her first vows in Adelaide in 2010. She has since studied a Bachelor of Theology, Graduate Diploma of Teaching and Learning, and Master of Theology (Coursework). Her ministries have been with youth, immigration detention centres, prisons, parish, school and ecumenical/interfaith relations. Her latest role is as a parish life coordinator in a remote community in the Diocese of Wilcannia-Forbes. Elizabeth finds life in exploring the scriptures and the Church's liturgical/sacramental tradition together with those in marginal situations.

# Acknowledgements

The Australian Women Preach Podcast and this book would not have been possible without the amazing support and creative work of many people.

We acknowledge:

- WATAC Inc. (Women and the Australian Church) and The Grail in Australia for their belief, encouragement, and financial support.

- Our incredible, hardworking, enthusiastic, and flexible podcast producer, Louise Maher.

- The composer of the inspirational music which accompanies the podcast, Danielle Anne Lynch.

- The connection to place, Spirit and Gospel poeticised by Di Langham and Belinda Roberts in the *Welcome to Country* and accompanying artwork, *Leaves on the Line*.

- The creative vision of Sophie Cole, who provided the image for the front cover of this book.

- All our amazing, talented and Spirit-filled preachers.

- The tireless and patient Karen Tayleur and the team at Garratt Publishing for pulling this book together.

- And last, but certainly not least, the Australian Women Preach organising team for their dedication to this project and raising women's voices in preaching the gospel: Rebecca Beisler, Andrea Dean, Patricia Gemmell, Elizabeth Lee, Tracy McEwan, Angela Marquis, Colleen Rowe, and Philippa Wicksey.

www.ingramcontent.com/pod-product-compliance
Lightning Source LLC
Chambersburg PA
CBHW072056110526
44590CB00018B/3194